Air Fry
Everything!

Meredith Laurence

Photography by Jessica Walker

Walah!, LLC Publishers
Philadelphia

First Edition

Published in the United States by Walah!, LLC/Publishers

walah@me.com

Library of Congress Cataloging-in-Publication Data

    Laurence, Meredith, author.
       Air fry everything / Meredith Laurence ; photography
    by Jessica Walker. -- First edition.
       pages cm
       Includes index.
       ISBN 978-0-9827540-4-7

       1. Hot air frying. 2. Cookbooks.   I. Title.

    TX689.L38 2016   641.7'7
                      QBI16-600089

Printed in USA

Book design by Janis Boehm
www.bound-determined.com

Photography by Jessica Walker
www.jessicawalkerphotography.com

Food styling by Lisa Ventura, Bonne Di Tomo and Lucille Osborn

Acknowledgments

As with any book project, I could not have done this alone. Or, if I did, this book would be much smaller, with no photographs, unbound and printed on copy paper. So, I have many people to thank for all the help and support they gave to me.

Huge thanks to my friend and assistant, Lisa Ventura, who helped with all the recipes, the photo shoot and by keeping everything looking beautiful. We may not work the same hours, but you never miss a deadline and never fail to support me in my most stressful moments! Thank you!

I'm forever grateful for the opportunities to work with my designer, Janis Boehm. Thank you for your focus on the details and for your patience with all my requests. It's rare to have as much fun as I do working with a friend like you.

Jessica Walker, you are a joy to work with and truly make the photo shoots so much fun. Your food photography is beautiful, and if I have to be on this side of the lens, I'm glad you're on the other!

My amazing food stylists - Bonne de Tomo and Lucille Osborn. Not everyone can mix work and laughter the way you do, *and* still get things done. Thank you.

Thank you to my oldest friend (as in longest known), Tanya van Biesen. You've always been my biggest cheerleader. Your enthusiasm to test recipes and your ability to sight typos, errors or just find a better way of saying things amazed me.

Penny Markowitz and my parents, Norma and Denys Laurence, graciously proofread every recipe with astonishing speed and accuracy. Thank you.

Big thanks also go out to Linda Lisco and Amy Nichols, who encourage and advise me, and keep me on the right road.

Eric Theiss, as always, kept the ship sailing while I was below deck writing, testing, eating and editing. You are always there for me to lean on when the seas get rough. Thank you.

Annie Symes. No one could have helped and supported me more, especially this year. This has been a long year for you too, but you tested, tasted, read through, read through again (and again) and kept me going. Never-ending thanks and love.

About this Book

I want this book and the recipes in it to be accessible to everyone. You'll find basic recipes here for the newcomer, as well as slightly more challenging recipes for those who want to take their air-frying to the next level. I believe that every recipe in this book is something anyone can make, but I've marked those recipes that are really easy with a "Super Easy" stamp.

In addition, I want to make sure that there are lots of options in this book for all kinds of cooks and so I included a vegetarian main dishes section, as well as included vegetarian recipes throughout the other sections of the book. All these recipes are marked with a "Vegetarian" stamp so you can identify them quickly.

I've added a new stamp to some of my recipes this time around, and have marked when a recipe is gluten-free. You'll see a "Gluten-Free" stamp on thirty-six recipes, however, there are many other recipes in the book that you can make gluten-free simply by buying gluten-free ingredients, such as gluten-free mayonnaise or gluten-free soy sauce. I take the gluten-free stamp very seriously, so any recipe that earned that stamp is sure to be gluten-free regardless of what brand or type of ingredient you buy.

Finally, I want you to know what my favorite recipes from the book are and I've marked those as "BJC Fav's".

The recipes in this book were tested with various brands and wattages of 3-quart air fryers. If you are using an air fryer that is larger than 3-quarts, then you're in luck. Where you might see instructions for cooking batches of food, you can probably save time and cook more at once. In addition, you might also find that you can shave a few minutes off the cooking time. Take a peek at the section Converting Recipes on page 16 for more information.

Regardless of what size air fryer you are using, understand that much like cooking in an oven or on the stovetop, timing may vary a little based on a number of factors – the size of your food (large chicken breasts versus smaller chicken breasts), the size of the cuts of foods, the temperature of your ingredients, etc… Use your better judgment when cooking to determine when foods are cooked to your liking. The great thing about an air fryer is that you can very easily remove the drawer at any time during the cooking process to see how things are going.

Table of Contents

Snacks and Appetizers

Breads and Breakfast

★ Blue Jean Chef Favorites   ■ Super Easy Recipes   ▼ Vegetarian   ● Gluten-Free

Vegetarian Main Dishes

Vegetables

Desserts

A Little More...

★ Blue Jean Chef Favorites   ■ Super Easy Recipes   ▼ Vegetarian   ● Gluten-Free

Foreword
David Venable

If you're like me, you're always looking for new and creative ways to get delicious food on the table. Food that is simple to prepare, family-friendly, and better for the ones we love. My friend Meredith Laurence, aka The Blue Jean Chef, has done just that with her new cookbook titled Air Fry Everything! It's a new collection of recipes featuring the air fryer to deliver crispy, mouthwatering results in a fraction of the time and with less fat and oil.

For 15 years on QVC, Meredith has been our teacher in the kitchen and her new cookbook delivers what we love to eat in record time. Having sold over 100,000 air fryers on QVC, I hear first-hand from our Foodies who are clamoring for more recipes for this unique appliance. In Air Fry Everything!, Meredith delivers what you've been asking for, with tasty favorites such as Buffalo Wings, Bacon Wrapped Filets, Fried Banana S'mores, and a special recipe I requested—Philly Chicken Cheesesteak Stromboli. It makes me want to do the "Happy Dance" just thinking about it.

Every page in the book and each one of the over 130 recipes will inspire you to think about your air fryer in a brand new way. More of my favorites include Puff Pastry Apples, Honey Mesquite Pork Chops, and Beer Battered Onion Rings. Meredith's energetic style is contagious and shines through in every delicious dish. As always, she makes you feel comfortable in the kitchen with her easy, confident approach to cooking and in this case, air frying!

Air Fry Everything! will become your go-to recipe collection for family dinners, parties, and everyday snacks. I know you'll enjoy every lip-smacking bite.

Keep it flavorful,
David Venable
Host, ***In The Kitchen with David***®
QVC

Introduction

I've been getting older these last few years. And as I get older, I find myself more resistant to new gadgets and gizmos, new devices and crazes. I guess many of us find ourselves changing in this way, but that is why it is astonishing that I have become absolutely besotted and enamored with air fryers. Air fryers are the latest greatest addition to the world of kitchen electronics, but they do sound a little gimmicky, and it is rather in the nature of a gimmick to be a passing fad without purpose. I'm not drawn to passing fads, so when I first heard about an air fryer, I doubted that it would be a useful tool for me in my kitchen. I had survived for so many years without one.

Then, I tried it. I made steak frites. The frites were pretty good (good enough to motivate me to tweak my technique to perfect them) and made with so little oil that I felt perfectly guilt-free. The steak, however, was outrageously good. Nicely browned and seared on the outside and so very juicy inside. It was so good that I was convinced that if only for cooking steaks, an air fryer would be a worthwhile investment. The air fryer had planted its hook in me.

So, I tried more things. The more I tried, the more I liked this new appliance – no longer a gimmick in my mind, but a useful, efficient and multi-purpose tool. Now, I can't imagine the inconvenience of being without one. It sits on my counter, next to my neglected and disgruntled oven, and is used daily, whether it's to make a full meal, or just to heat leftovers, or toast some bread or make quick croutons. It's quick, efficient and effective. If it were applying for a job in my kitchen, it would be hired on the spot!

As the Blue Jean Chef, I share most of what I do in the kitchen with people because I am passionate about helping people be successful and comfortable in their kitchens – as comfortable as they'd be in their blue jeans. And so, I am sharing my new passion with you again – this time in the form of air-frying. It's easy, it's fun, it's quick and it gives great results. What sort of person would I be if I held that from you? ☺

If You are Brand New to Air Frying...

Air Frying Basics

In the simplest of terms, an air-fryer is a compact cylindrical countertop convection oven. It's a kitchen appliance that uses superheated air to cook foods, giving results very similar to deep-frying or high-temperature roasting. Many of us have convection ovens in our kitchens. In a standard oven, air is heated and the hot air cooks the food. In a convection oven, air is heated and then blown around by a fan. This creates more energy and consequently cooks foods faster and more evenly. Air fryers use the same technology as convection ovens, but instead of blowing the air around a large rectangular box, it is blown around in a compact cylinder and the food sits in a perforated basket. This is much more efficient and creates an intense environment of heat from which the food cannot escape. The result is food with a crispy brown exterior and moist tender interior – results similar to deep-frying, but without all the oil and fat needed to deep-fry. In fact, when you are air-frying, you usually use no more than one tablespoon of oil!

Better still, an air fryer doesn't just cook foods that you would usually deep-fry. It can cook any foods that you would normally cook in your oven or microwave as well. It is a great tool for re-heating foods without making them rubbery, and is a perfect and quick way to prepare ingredients as well as make meals. To me, it is the best new kitchen appliance that has been introduced in recent years.

Health Benefits

Obviously, because it can produce results similar to deep-frying using a tiny fraction of the oil needed to deep-fry, the health benefits are apparent. When deep-frying, you submerge the food in oil and oil is inevitably absorbed by the food. In an air fryer, you still use oil because oil is what helps crisp and brown many foods, but you really don't need more than one table-spoon at a time. Instead of putting the tablespoon of oil in the air fryer, you simply toss foods with oil and then place them in the air fryer basket. In fact, spraying the foods lightly with oil is an even easier way to get foods evenly coated with the least amount of oil. Investing in a kitchen spray bottle is a great idea if you have an air fryer.

Quick and Energy Efficient

We all know that sometimes it can take fifteen to twenty minutes to pre-heat our standard ovens. Because the air fryer is so compact, that pre-heat time is cut down to two or three minutes! That's a huge savings in time as well as energy. In the summer, you can pre-heat your air fryer and not heat up the whole kitchen. In addition, the intense heat created in the air fryer cooks foods quickly, about 20% faster than in an oven, so you're saving time and energy there as well. No one these days seems to have time to spare, so this should please everyone!

Safe and Easy to Use

Air-frying is safer and easier than deep-frying. Most air fryers have settings for time and temperature. You simply enter both and press start. It doesn't get much easier than that! When deep-frying, you have to heat a large pot of oil on the stovetop, use a deep-frying thermometer to register the temperature and then monitor the heat below the pot to maintain that temperature. On top of it all, you are dealing with a lot of oil, which can be heavy to move, dangerous if it gets too hot, and is cumbersome and annoying to drain and dispose of. Why bother if you can get the same results so much more easily with an air fryer?

Clean and Tidy

I didn't earn the "Miss Tidy Bed" badge in brownies for no reason! I love keeping the kitchen clean and tidy when I'm cooking and after I've been cooking. The air fryer fits into my world perfectly. It cooks foods in a contained space and that keeps the food from splattering anywhere. Period. It is simple and straightforward to clean and keep clean, and you know what they say about cleanliness...😊

Using Air Fryers to Prepare Ingredients

So often, I find myself turning to the air fryer to cook ingredients for meals that might not even call for an air fryer. Don't underestimate the convenience of quickly toasting some nuts for a salad, or roasting a pepper for pasta, or quickly cooking bacon for an egg sandwich. Ingredients in recipes often come with a qualifier – "walnuts, toasted", or "bread cubes, toasted" – and the air fryer comes to the rescue, once again saving precious time.

Converting Recipes

Converting From Traditional Recipes

You can use your air fryer to cook recipes that have instructions for cooking in the oven. Because the heat in the air fryer is more intense than a standard oven, reduce the suggested temperature by 25°F – 50°F and cut the time by roughly 20%. So, if a recipe calls for cooking at 400°F for 20 minutes, air-fry at 370°F for about 16 minutes. You can also refer to the cooking charts in this book on page 238 to help determine the right cooking time for foods. Remember to turn foods over halfway through the cooking time (as you would in a skillet or on the grill) and check the foods for your desired degree of doneness as you approach the finish line.

Converting From Packaged Foods Instructions

The same rule applies to prepared foods that you might buy at the grocery store. If a bag of frozen French fries suggests cooking in the oven at 450°F for 18 minutes, air fry the fries at 400°F and start checking them at 15 minutes, remembering to shake the basket once or twice during the cooking process to help the fries brown evenly.

Converting to Different Sized Air-Fryers

Larger air fryers can make life a little easier, especially if you're cooking for 4 or more people. Because the baskets in these air fryers are larger, you can cook more food at one time and do not have to cook the food in batches as specified in many of these recipes. Just remember not to over-fill the air fryer basket, since that will just slow down the overall cooking time and result in foods that are not as crispy as you'd like them to be.

In addition, some larger air fryers with more power might cook foods slightly faster than smaller, lower wattage air fryers. This will not be a significant difference, but might save you a couple of minutes on some recipes. As with all things you cook in the air fryer, it makes sense to pull open the air fryer drawer and check the foods as they cook. That way, you'll avoid over-cooking anything.

General Tips for Air-Frying

Preparing to air-fry

- **Find the right place for your air fryer in your kitchen.** Always keep your air fryer on a level, heat-resistant countertop and make sure there are at least five inches of space behind the air fryer where the exhaust vent is located.

- **Pre-heat your air fryer before adding your food.** This is easy – just turn the air fryer on to the temperature that you need and set the timer for 2 or 3 minutes. When the timer goes off, the air fryer has pre-heated and is ready for food.

- **Invest in a kitchen spray bottle.** Spraying oil on the food is easier than drizzling or brushing, and allows you to use less oil overall. While you can buy oil sprays in cans, sometimes there are aerosol agents in those cans that can break down the non-stick surface on your air fryer basket. So, if you want to spray foods directly in the basket, invest in a hand-pumped kitchen spray bottle. It will be worth it!

- **Use the proper breading technique.** Breading is an important step in many air fryer recipes. Don't skip a step! It is important to coat foods with flour first, then egg and then the breadcrumbs. Be diligent about the breadcrumbs and press them onto the food with your hands. Because the air fryer has a powerful fan as part of its mechanism, breading can sometimes blow off the food. Pressing those crumbs on firmly will help the breading adhere.

- **Get the right accessories.** Once you start air frying, you may want to invest in some accessories for your new favorite appliance. Truth is, you may already have some! Any baking dishes or cake pans that are oven-safe should be air fryer-safe as well, as long as they don't come in contact with the heating element. The only stipulation, of course, is that the accessory pan has to be able to fit inside the air fryer basket.

- **Use an aluminum foil sling.** Getting accessory pieces into and out of the air fryer basket can be tricky. To make it easier, fold a piece of aluminum foil into a strip about 2-inches wide by 24-inches long. Place the cake pan or baking dish on the foil and by holding the ends of the foil, you'll be able to lift the pan or dish and lower it into the air fryer basket. Fold or tuck the ends of the aluminum foil into the air fryer basket, and then return the basket to the air fryer. When you're ready to remove the pan, unfold and hold onto the ends of the aluminum foil to lift the pan out of the air fryer basket.

General Tips for Air-Frying

While you are air-frying

- **Add water to the air fryer drawer when cooking fatty foods.** Adding water to the drawer underneath the basket helps prevent grease from getting too hot and smoking. Do this when cooking bacon, sausage, even burgers if they are particularly fatty.

- **Use toothpicks to hold foods down.** Every once in a while, the fan from the air fryer will pick up light foods and blow them around. So, secure foods (like the top slice of bread on a sandwich) with toothpicks.

- **Don't overcrowd the basket.** I can't stress this enough. It's tempting to try to cook more at one time, but over-crowding the basket will prevent foods from crisping and browning evenly and take more time over all.

- **Flip foods over halfway through the cooking time.** Just as you would if you were cooking on a grill or in a skillet, you need to turn foods over so that they brown evenly.

- **Open the air fryer as often as you like to check for doneness.** This is one of the best parts of air fryers – you can open that drawer as often as you like (within reason) to check to see how the cooking process is coming along. This will not interrupt the timing of most air fryers – the fryer will either continue heating and timing as you pull the basket out, or pick up where it left off when you return the basket to the fryer.

- **Shake the basket.** Shaking the basket a couple of times during the cooking process will re-distribute the ingredients and help them to brown and crisp more evenly.

- **Spray with oil part way through.** If you are trying to get the food to brown and crisp more, try spritzing it with oil part way through the cooking process. This will also help the food to brown more evenly.

After you air-fry

- **Remove the air fryer basket from the drawer before turning out foods.** This is very important and it's a mistake you'll only make once. 😵 If you invert the basket while it is still locked into the air fryer drawer, you will end up dumping all the rendered fat or excess grease onto your plate along with the food you just air-fried.

- **Don't pour away the juices from the drawer too soon.** The drawer below the air fryer basket collects a lot of juices from the cooked foods above and catches any marinades that you pour over the food. If the drippings are not too greasy, you can use this flavorful liquid as a sauce to pour over the food. You can also de-grease this liquid and reduce it in a small saucepan on the stovetop for a few minutes to concentrate the flavor.

- **Clean the drawer as well as the basket after every use.** The drawer of the air fryer is very easy to clean, so don't put it off. If you leave it unwashed, you'll run the risk of food contamination and your kitchen won't smell very nice in a day or so!
- **Use the air fryer to dry itself.** After washing the air fryer basket and drawer, just pop them back into the air fryer and turn it on for 2 or 3 minutes. That dries both parts better than any drying towel.

Re-heating foods in the air-fryer

- **There's no hard and fast rule for time and temperature when re-heating leftovers because leftovers vary so significantly.** I suggest re-heating in the air fryer at 350°F and doing so for as long as it takes for the food to be re-heated to a food safety temperature of 165°F. This is especially important for any potentially hazardous foods like chicken, pork and beef.

Trouble-shooting

- **Food is not getting crispy enough.** Make sure you are not over-crowding the air fryer basket and make sure you are using just a little oil.
- **There is white smoke coming from the air fryer.** Add some water to the air fryer drawer underneath the basket. The white smoke is probably because grease has drained into the drawer and is burning. Adding water will prevent this.
- **There is black smoke coming from the air fryer.** Turn the machine off and look up towards the heating element inside the fryer. Some food might have blown up and attached to the heating element, burning and causing the black smoke.
- **The air fryer won't turn off.** Many air fryers are designed to have a delay in their shutting down process. Once you press the power button off, the fan will continue to blow the hot air out of the unit for about 20 seconds. Don't press the power button again, or you will have just turned the machine back on. Be patient and wait, and the air fryer will turn off.

Recipe Rules

In every cooking class I've ever taught, I try to set people up for success by setting some ground rules. Sounds strict, but it really isn't. I prefer to think of these rules as helpful hints.

First rule – read the recipe from start to finish before you begin cooking. This is critical in order to know if you have all the ingredients, as well as if you have enough time to complete the recipe.

Second rule – buy the very best ingredients you can. A finished dish can only taste as good as its ingredients.

Third rule – do your mise en place. This means do all your prep work first. Chop what needs to be chopped. Measure what needs to be measured. This makes cooking much less stressful and more relaxing. Of course, you can start a step of the recipe in the middle of doing your mise en place if that first step in the recipe requires some time. You'll know this because you will have read the recipe all the way through first!

Fourth rule – taste your food before you take it to the table. You'd be surprised how many people forget this step, but it's really important. You should always take a few seconds to taste the food and re-season it if necessary.

Specifics about Ingredients

- **Onions, Garlic and Carrots.** Unless you enjoy eating the skin and peels of these vegetables, assume that they should always be peeled.

- **Potatoes.** I specify whether or not to peel the potatoes before using them in the recipes. If it   doesn't say "peeled" that means wash the potatoes, but leave the skins on.

- **Chicken.** Most of the time, I will let you know if the chicken called for in a recipe includes skin or is skinless, includes bones or is boneless. If I don't specify, it's entirely up to you!

- **Breadcrumbs.** There are a lot of different types of breadcrumbs used in this cookbook. Panko breadcrumbs are made from a crust-less white bread (although you can find a tan variety that is made with the crusts) and are lighter, flakier and crispier than regular breadcrumbs. Because they resist absorbing oils, they will give you a crispier finish. Plain or fresh breadcrumbs are made from fresh bread and produce a softer coating or crust. Toasted or dried breadcrumbs are made from bread that has been previously toasted and consequently will give you a crispier coating than fresh breadcrumbs, but not as crispy as panko breadcrumbs.

- **Good quality ingredients**. Sometimes you will see instructions to use "Parmigiano-Reggiano cheese" rather than just Parmesan cheese. While I strongly recommend using the very best ingredients all the time, sometimes an ingredient has extra importance in a recipe and absolutely must be of the highest quality. If you see "good quality" listed beside an ingredient, then you'll know that you can't substitute an inferior quality in its place and expect the same excellent results.

I may call them rules, but all of these points are just to set you off on the right path!

If you would like to learn more about air-frying, or would like more recipes for your air-fryer and other cooking tools, please visit me at www.bluejeanchef.com.

Snacks and Appetizers

Charred Shishito Peppers

You can't find shishito peppers in every grocery store yet, but if you do see them, be sure to grab some! A shishito pepper is a small finger-sized pepper that is usually mild and sweet, but every one in ten peppers has some kick to it. It makes for a fun and exciting appetizer snack – sort of like snack roulette!

Serves
4

Temperature
390°F

Cooking Time
5 minutes

20 shishito peppers (about 6 ounces)

1 teaspoon vegetable oil

coarse sea salt

1 lemon

1. Pre-heat the air fryer to 390ºF.

2. Toss the shishito peppers with the oil and salt. You can do this in a bowl or directly in the air fryer basket.

3. Air-fry at 390ºF for 5 minutes, shaking the basket once or twice while they cook.

4. Turn the charred peppers out into a bowl. Squeeze some lemon juice over the top and season with coarse sea salt. These should be served as finger foods – pick the pepper up by the stem and eat the whole pepper, seeds and all. Watch for that surprise spicy one!

Dress It Up

You can dress these peppers up by serving them with a cool dip like a cucumber raita. Mix together 1 cup of grated cucumber, 1 cup of plain yogurt, ½ teaspoon ground cumin, ¼ teaspoon ground coriander, 3 tablespoons chopped fresh mint, 1 tablespoon lemon juice, salt and freshly ground black pepper.

Crispy Spiced Chickpeas

Careful... these are addictive! You'll be making another batch before you know it!

Serves
2 to 4

Temperature
400°F

Cooking Time
15 to 20 minutes

1 (15-ounce) can chickpeas, drained (or 1½ cups cooked chickpeas)

½ teaspoon salt

½ teaspoon chili powder

¼ teaspoon ground cinnamon

⅛ teaspoon smoked paprika

pinch ground cayenne pepper

1 tablespoon olive oil

1. Pre-heat the air fryer to 400°F.

2. Dry the chickpeas as well as you can with a clean kitchen towel, rubbing off any loose skins as necessary. Combine the spices in a small bowl. Toss the chickpeas with the olive oil and then add the spices and toss again.

3. Air-fry for 15 minutes, shaking the basket a couple of times while they cook.

4. Check the chickpeas to see if they are crispy enough and if necessary, air-fry for another 5 minutes to crisp them further. Serve warm, or cool to room temperature and store in an airtight container for up to two weeks.

Substitution

You can really vary this recipe by using different spices to season the chickpeas. Try curry powder instead of chili powder for a change of pace.

Buffalo Wings

Get the napkins ready because you know you're going to need 'em! These wings marinate in the hot sauce and then you toss them with more hot sauce at the end. They can't help but be super flavorful, even without deep frying in oil.

Serves
2

Temperature
400°F

Cooking Time
22 minutes
(10 minutes per batch plus 2 minutes)

2 pounds chicken wings

3 tablespoons butter, melted

¼ cup hot sauce
(like Crystal® or Frank's®)

Finishing Sauce:

3 tablespoons butter, melted

¼ cup hot sauce
(like Crystal® or Frank's®)

1 teaspoon Worcestershire sauce

1. Prepare the chicken wings by cutting off the wing tips and discarding (or freezing for chicken stock). Divide the drumettes from the wingettes by cutting through the joint. Place the chicken wing pieces in a large bowl.

2. Combine the melted butter and the hot sauce and stir to blend well. Pour the marinade over the chicken wings, cover and let the wings marinate for 2 hours or up to overnight in the refrigerator.

3. Pre-heat the air fryer to 400ºF.

4. Air-fry the wings in two batches for 10 minutes per batch, shaking the basket halfway through the cooking process. When both batches are done, toss all the wings back into the basket for another 2 minutes to heat through and finish cooking.

5. While the wings are air-frying, combine the remaining 3 tablespoons of butter, ¼ cup of hot sauce and the Worcestershire sauce. Remove the wings from the air fryer, toss them in the finishing sauce and serve with some cooling blue cheese dip and celery sticks.

Buffalo wings at your average fast food restaurant have roughly 670 calories per serving. Because we don't deep-fry these wings, we can save ourselves about 250 calories!

420 Calories – 34g Fat – (15g Sat. Fat) – 1g Carbohydrates
0g Fiber – 1g Sugar – 27g Protein

Cherry Chipotle BBQ Chicken Wings

This cherry chipotle BBQ sauce is so easy to make, and yet it really sets these wings apart from your regular chicken wings. A quick and easy dry rub at the beginning also helps to enhance the flavor.

Serves
2

Temperature
400°F

Cooking Time
22 minutes
(10 minutes per batch plus 2 minutes)

1 teaspoon smoked paprika

½ teaspoon dry mustard powder

1 teaspoon dried oregano

1 teaspoon dried thyme

½ teaspoon chili powder

1 teaspoon salt

2 pounds chicken wings

vegetable oil or spray

salt and freshly ground black pepper

1 to 2 tablespoons chopped chipotle peppers in adobo sauce

⅓ cup cherry preserves

¼ cup tomato ketchup

1. Combine the first six ingredients in a large bowl. Prepare the chicken wings by cutting off the wing tips and discarding (or freezing for chicken stock). Divide the drumettes from the wingettes by cutting through the joint. Place the chicken wing pieces in the bowl with the spice mix. Toss or shake well to coat.

2. Pre-heat the air fryer to 400°F.

3. Spray the wings lightly with the vegetable oil and air-fry the wings in two batches for 10 minutes per batch, shaking the basket halfway through the cooking process. When both batches are done, toss all the wings back into the basket for another 2 minutes to heat through and finish cooking.

4. While the wings are air-frying, combine the chopped chipotle peppers, cherry preserves and ketchup in a bowl.

5. Remove the wings from the air fryer, toss them in the cherry chipotle BBQ sauce and serve with napkins!

Did You Know...?

A chipotle is a dried and smoked Jalapeño pepper. Adobo sauce is a combination of paprika, spices and vinegar used to preserve the chipotles. The Adobo sauce takes on the flavor of the chipotles and becomes a really flavorful ingredient. Don't forget to use it too!

Honey-Mustard Chicken Wings

These wings can be as sweet or as spicy as you want them to be. If you're looking for a little kick, use a spicy mustard with lots of mustard seeds.

Serves
2

Temperature
400°F

Cooking Time
24 minutes
(10 minutes per batch plus 4 minutes)

2 pounds chicken wings

salt and freshly ground black pepper

2 tablespoons butter

¼ cup honey

¼ cup spicy brown mustard

pinch ground cayenne pepper

2 teaspoons Worcestershire sauce

1. Prepare the chicken wings by cutting off the wing tips and discarding (or freezing for chicken stock). Divide the drumettes from the wingettes by cutting through the joint. Place the chicken wing pieces in a large bowl.

2. Pre-heat the air fryer to 400°F.

3. Season the wings with salt and freshly ground black pepper and air-fry the wings in two batches for 10 minutes per batch, shaking the basket half way through the cooking process.

4. While the wings are air-frying, combine the remaining ingredients in a small saucepan over low heat.

5. When both batches are done, toss all the wings with the honey-mustard sauce and toss them all back into the basket for another 4 minutes to heat through and finish cooking. Give the basket a good shake part way through the cooking process to redistribute the wings. Remove the wings from the air fryer and serve.

You can buy chicken wings that have already been separated into drumettes and wingettes, but wings that are sold whole tend to be meatier and more plump. So, pick up the whole wings and brush up on your knife skills!

Popcorn Chicken Bites

This is a simple snack that will keep away the hunger pangs. It's easy, but oh so snackable!

Serves
2 to 4

Temperature
380°F

Cooking Time
16 minutes
(8 minutes per batch)

1 pound chicken breasts, cutlets
or tenders

1 cup buttermilk

3 to 6 dashes hot sauce (optional)

8 cups cornflakes
(or 2 cups cornflake crumbs)

½ teaspoon salt

1 tablespoon butter, melted

2 tablespoons chopped fresh parsley

1. Cut the chicken into bite-sized pieces (about 1-inch) and place them in a bowl with the buttermilk and hot sauce (if using). Cover and let the chicken marinate in the buttermilk for 1 to 3 hours in the refrigerator.

2. Pre-heat the air fryer to 380°F.

3. Crush the cornflakes into fine crumbs by either crushing them with your hands in a bowl, rolling them with a rolling pin in a plastic bag or processing them in a food processor. Place the crumbs in a bowl, add the salt, melted butter and parsley and mix well. Working in batches, remove the chicken from the buttermilk marinade, letting any excess drip off and transfer the chicken to the cornflakes. Toss the chicken pieces in the cornflake mixture to coat evenly, pressing the crumbs onto the chicken.

4. Air-fry the chicken in two batches for 8 minutes per batch, shaking the basket halfway through the cooking process. Re-heat the first batch with the second batch for a couple of minutes if desired.

5. Serve the popcorn chicken bites warm with BBQ sauce or honey mustard for dipping.

Did you know that you can buy cornflake crumbs in the grocery store? They're sitting right there next to the breadcrumbs!

Beer Battered Onion Rings

Many people consider onion rings a guilty pleasure. Well, these ones aren't so guilty!

Serves
2 to 4

Temperature
360°F

Cooking Time
16 minutes

⅔ cup flour

½ teaspoon baking soda

1 teaspoon paprika

1 teaspoon salt

½ teaspoon freshly ground black pepper

¾ cup beer

1 egg, beaten

1½ cups fine breadcrumbs

1 large Vidalia onion, peeled and sliced into ½-inch rings

vegetable oil

1. Set up a dredging station. Mix the flour, baking soda, paprika, salt and pepper together in a bowl. Pour in the beer, add the egg and whisk until smooth. Place the breadcrumbs in a cake pan or shallow dish.

2. Separate the onion slices into individual rings. Dip each onion ring into the batter with a fork. Lift the onion ring out of the batter and let any excess batter drip off. Then place the onion ring in the breadcrumbs and shake the cake pan back and forth to coat the battered onion ring. Pat the ring gently with your hands to make sure the breadcrumbs stick and that both sides of the ring are covered. Place the coated onion ring on a sheet pan and repeat with the rest of the onion rings.

3. Pre-heat the air fryer to 360°F.

4. Lightly spray the onion rings with oil, coating both sides. Layer the onion rings in the air fryer basket, stacking them on top of each other in a haphazard manner.

5. Air-fry for 10 minutes at 360°F. Flip the onion rings over and rotate the onion rings from the bottom of the basket to the top. Air-fry for an additional 6 minutes.

6. Serve immediately with your favorite dipping sauce, or try the dipping sauce from the Blooming Onion on page 58.

Substitution

If you don't want to use beer in this recipe try substituting milk.

Smart Tip

Onion rings in the average fast food restaurant have roughly 530 calories. This less-guilty version comes in at 140 calories.

140 Calories – 0.5g Fat – (0g Sat Fat) – 31g Carbohydrates
4g Fiber – 3g Sugar – 4g Protein

Homemade French Fries

I made French fries so many different ways with the air fryer until I settled on this method. What I like about these French fries is that they are crispy and brown on the outside, but tender and steamy on the inside. Potato perfection!

Serves
2 to 3

Temperature
400°F

Cooking Time
25 minutes

2 to 3 russet potatoes, peeled and cut into ½-inch sticks

2 to 3 teaspoons olive or vegetable oil

salt

1. Bring a large saucepan of salted water to a boil on the stovetop while you peel and cut the potatoes. Blanch the potatoes in the boiling salted water for 4 minutes while you pre-heat the air fryer to 400ºF. Strain the potatoes and rinse them with cold water. Dry them well with a clean kitchen towel.

2. Toss the dried potato sticks gently with the oil and place them in the air fryer basket. Air-fry for 25 minutes, shaking the basket a few times while the fries cook to help them brown evenly. Season the fries with salt mid-way through cooking and serve them warm with tomato ketchup, Sriracha mayonnaise or a mix of lemon zest, Parmesan cheese and parsley. Yum!

Smart Tip

French fries at the average fast food restaurant have roughly 230 calories per serving. In addition, they can have many "extra" ingredients. These delicious fries have only 133 calories for the same size serving and only three ingredients – potatoes, salt and a little oil.

130 Calories – 0g Fat – (0g Sat. Fat) – 30g Carbohydrates
2g Fiber – 1g Sugar – 4g Protein

Skinny Fries

As much as I'd like to believe I could eat as many of these as I want to and become skinny, that's not quite true. The fries themselves, however, are skinny and use a different technique to the Homemade French Fries.

Serves
2

Temperature
380°F

Cooking Time
30 minutes
(15 minutes per batch)

2 to 3 russet potatoes, peeled and cut into ¼-inch sticks

2 to 3 teaspoons olive or vegetable oil

salt

1. Cut the potatoes into ¼-inch strips. (A mandolin with a julienne blade is really helpful here.) Rinse the potatoes with cold water several times and let them soak in cold water for at least 10 minutes or as long as overnight.

2. Pre-heat the air fryer to 380°F.

3. Drain and dry the potato sticks really well, using a clean kitchen towel. Toss the fries with the oil in a bowl and then air-fry the fries in two batches at 380°F for 15 minutes, shaking the basket a couple of times while they cook.

4. Add the first batch of French fries back into the air fryer basket with the finishing batch and let everything warm through for a few minutes. As soon as the fries are done, season them with salt and transfer to a plate or basket. Serve them warm with ketchup or your favorite dip.

Poutine

*Canada's favorite way to eat French fries! While you can eat these with your fingers,
I highly recommend grabbing a fork!*

Serves
2

Temperature
400°F

Cooking Time
25 minutes

BIG FAV

2 russet potatoes, scrubbed
and cut into ½-inch sticks

2 teaspoons vegetable oil

2 tablespoons butter

¼ onion, minced (about ¼ cup)

1 clove garlic, smashed

¼ teaspoon dried thyme

3 tablespoons flour

1 teaspoon tomato paste

1½ cups strong beef stock

salt and lots of freshly ground
black pepper

a few dashes of Worcestershire sauce

⅔ cup chopped string cheese or
cheese curds

1. Bring a large saucepan of salted water to a boil on the stovetop while you peel and cut the potatoes. Blanch the potatoes in the boiling salted water for 4 minutes while you pre-heat the air fryer to 400ºF. Strain the potatoes and rinse them with cold water. Dry them well with a clean kitchen towel.

2. Toss the dried potato sticks gently with the oil and place them in the air fryer basket. Air-fry for 25 minutes, shaking the basket a few times while the fries cook to help them brown evenly.

3. While the fries are cooking, make the gravy. Melt the butter in a small saucepan over medium heat. Add the onion, garlic and thyme and cook for five minutes, until soft and just starting to brown. Stir in the flour and cook for another two minutes, stirring regularly. Finally, add the tomato paste and continue to cook for another minute or two. Whisk in the beef stock and bring the mixture to a boil to thicken. Season to taste with salt, lots of freshly ground black pepper and a few dashes of Worcestershire sauce. Keep the gravy warm.

4. As soon as the fries are done, season them with salt and transfer to a plate or basket. Top the fries with the cheese curds or string cheese, and pour the warm gravy over the top. Grab a fork and get busy!

Parmesan French Fries

Once you have your French fry technique down, you can vary them in any number of ways – Parmesan cheese is one of my favorite variations!

Serves
2 to 3

Temperature
400°F

Cooking Time
25 minutes

2 to 3 large russet potatoes, peeled and cut into ½-inch sticks

2 teaspoons vegetable or canola oil

¾ cup grated Parmesan cheese

½ teaspoon salt

freshly ground black pepper

1 teaspoon fresh chopped parsley

1. Bring a large saucepan of salted water to a boil on the stovetop while you peel and cut the potatoes. Blanch the potatoes in the boiling salted water for 4 minutes while you pre-heat the air fryer to 400°F. Strain the potatoes and rinse them with cold water. Dry them well with a clean kitchen towel.

2. Toss the dried potato sticks gently with the oil and place them in the air fryer basket. Air-fry for 25 minutes, shaking the basket a few times while the fries cook to help them brown evenly.

3. Combine the Parmesan cheese, salt and pepper. With 2 minutes left on the air fryer cooking time, sprinkle the fries with the Parmesan cheese mixture. Toss the fries to coat them evenly with the cheese mixture and continue to air-fry for the final 2 minutes, until the cheese has melted and just starts to brown. Sprinkle the finished fries with chopped parsley, a little more grated Parmesan cheese if you like, and serve.

You can also make Parmesan French Fries using skinny fries. Just follow the Skinny Fries recipe on page 36 and toss the Parmesan mixture in at the end.

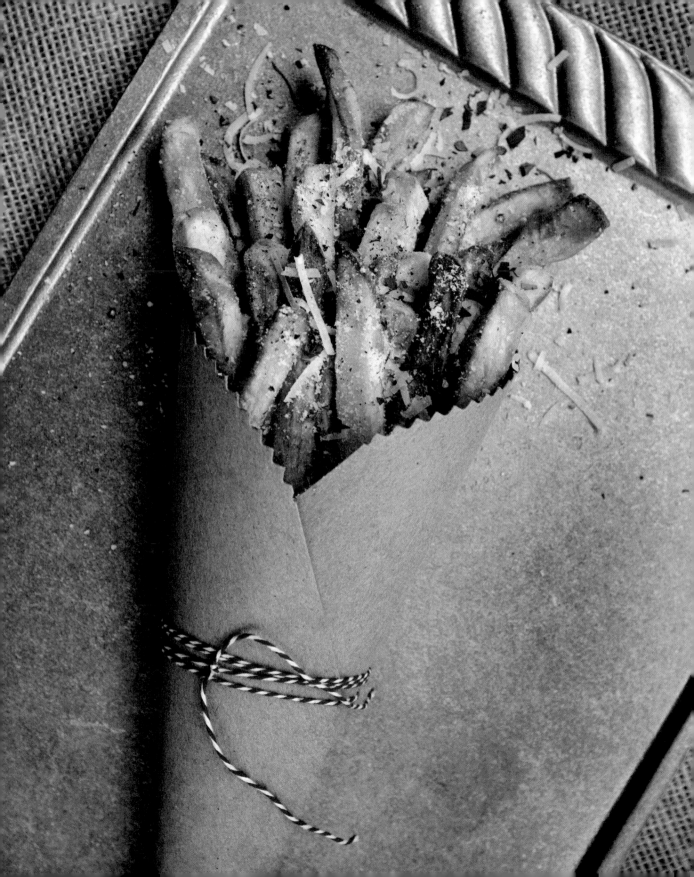

Crabby Fries

It's a Philly thing! Crab Fries are well known in Philadelphia, made famous by a restaurant chain called Chickie's & Pete's®. Crabby Fries are delicious, seasoned with Old Bay® Seasoning and served with a white cheese sauce dip.

Serves
2 to 3

Temperature
400°F

Cooking Time
30 minutes

2 to 3 large russet potatoes,
peeled and cut into ½-inch sticks

2 tablespoons vegetable oil

2 tablespoons butter

2 tablespoons flour

1 to 1½ cups milk

½ cup grated white Cheddar cheese

pinch of nutmeg

½ teaspoon salt

freshly ground black pepper

1 tablespoon Old Bay® Seasoning

1. Bring a large saucepan of salted water to a boil on the stovetop while you peel and cut the potatoes. Blanch the potatoes in the boiling salted water for 4 minutes while you pre-heat the air fryer to 400°F. Strain the potatoes and rinse them with cold water. Dry them well with a clean kitchen towel.

2. Toss the dried potato sticks gently with the oil and place them in the air fryer basket. Air-fry for 25 minutes, shaking the basket a few times while the fries cook to help them brown evenly.

3. While the fries are cooking, melt the butter in a medium saucepan. Whisk in the flour and cook for one minute. Slowly add 1 cup of milk, whisking constantly. Bring the mixture to a simmer and continue to whisk until it thickens. Remove the pan from the heat and stir in the Cheddar cheese. Add a pinch of nutmeg and season with salt and freshly ground black pepper. Transfer the warm cheese sauce to a serving dish. Thin with more milk if you want the sauce a little thinner.

4. As soon as the French fries have finished air-frying transfer them to a large bowl and season them with the Old Bay® Seasoning. Return the fries to the air fryer basket and air-fry for an additional 3 to 5 minutes. Serve immediately with the warm white Cheddar cheese sauce.

 Smart Tip

Crabby Fries are not part of a weight loss program!
Still, the same French fry dish out at a restaurant chain
would have 610 calories. This version saves you 120
calories with just 490 calories, sauce and all!

490 Calories – 24g Fat – (14g Sat. Fat) – 55g Carbohydrates
3g Fiber – 8g Sugar – 17g Protein

Spanakopita
Spinach, Feta and Pine Nut Phyllo Bites

Working with Phyllo dough can be a bit tricky. The most important thing to remember is to keep the dough from drying out, so cover the sheets you're not using with some plastic wrap or a damp clean kitchen towel. The beauty of Phyllo dough is that if it rips, don't fret – just patch it back together or cover it with another sheet.

Serves
8 to 10

Temperature
350°F

Cooking Time
30 minutes
(10 minutes per batch)

½ (10-ounce) package frozen spinach, thawed and squeezed dry (about 1 cup)

¾ cup crumbled feta cheese

¼ cup grated Parmesan cheese

¼ cup pine nuts, toasted

⅛ teaspoon ground nutmeg

1 egg, lightly beaten

½ teaspoon salt

freshly ground black pepper

6 sheets phyllo dough

½ cup butter, melted

1. Combine the spinach, cheeses, pine nuts, nutmeg and egg in a bowl. Season with salt and freshly ground black pepper.

2. While building the phyllo triangles, always keep the dough sheets you are not working with covered with plastic wrap and a damp clean kitchen towel. Remove one sheet of the phyllo and place it on a flat surface. Brush the phyllo sheet with melted butter and then layer another sheet of phyllo on top. Brush the second sheet of phyllo with butter. Cut the layered phyllo sheets into 6 strips, about 2½- to 3-inches wide.

3. Place a heaping tablespoon of the spinach filling at the end of each strip of dough. Fold the bottom right corner of the strip over the filling towards the left edge of the strip to make a triangle. Continue to fold the phyllo dough around the spinach as you would fold a flag, making triangle after triangle. Brush the outside of the phyllo triangle with more melted butter and set it aside until you've finished the 6 strips of dough, making 6 triangles.

4. Pre-heat the air fryer to 350°F.

5. Transfer the first six phyllo triangles to the air fryer basket and air-fry for 5 minutes. Turn the triangles over and air-fry for another 5 minutes.

6. While the first batch of triangles is air-frying, build another set of triangles and air-fry in the same manner. You should do three batches total. These can be warmed in the air fryer for a minute or two just before serving if you like.

Did You Know...?

You can toast the pinenuts in the air fryer. Place them in the air fryer and air-fry for 3 to 5 minutes at 350°F.

Potato Chips
with Sour Cream and Onion Dip

Of course you should be using your air fryer to make potato chips! Here, instead of having sour cream and onion chips, we have chips with sour cream and onion dip!

Serves
2 to 4

Temperature
300°F

Cooking Time
15 to 20 minutes

2 large potatoes (Yukon Gold or russet)

vegetable or olive oil in a spray bottle

sea salt and freshly ground black pepper

Sour Cream and Onion Dip:

½ cup sour cream

1 tablespoon olive oil

2 scallions, white part only minced

¼ teaspoon salt

freshly ground black pepper

a squeeze of lemon juice
(about ¼ teaspoon)

1. Wash the potatoes well, but leave the skins on. Slice them into ⅛-inch thin slices, using a mandolin or food processor. Rinse the potatoes under cold water until the water runs clear and then let them soak in a bowl of cold water for at least 10 minutes. Drain and dry the potato slices really well in a single layer on a clean kitchen towel.

2. Pre-heat the air fryer to 300°F. Spray the potato chips with the oil so that both sides are evenly coated, or rub the slices between your hands with some oil if you don't have a spray bottle.

3. Air-fry in two batches at 300°F for 15 to 20 minutes, shaking the basket a few times during the cooking process so the chips crisp and brown more evenly. Season the finished chips with sea salt and freshly ground black pepper while they are still hot.

4. While the chips are air-frying, make the sour cream and onion dip by mixing together the sour cream, olive oil, scallions, salt, pepper and lemon juice. Serve the chips warm or at room temperature along with the dip.

Did You Know...?

Even if your knife skills are great, you'd be best off with a mandolin slicer or food processor to make chips thin enough for this recipe. If you are using your chef's knife, and the chips are closer to ¼-inch thick, increase the time to about 30 to 40 minutes.

Chips and Dip
290 Calories – 16g Fat – (15.5g Sat. Fat) – 32g Carbohydrates
2g Fiber – 3g Sugar – 4g Protein

Chips alone
140 Calories – 4g Fat – (0g Sat. Fat) – 27g Carbohydrates
2g Fiber – 1g Sugar – 2g Protein

Grilled Ham & Muenster Cheese on Raisin Bread

Muenster cheese is an American semi-soft cheese with a relatively mild flavor, but it pairs so nicely with the honey ham and the sweet raisin bread. Best of all, it's a great melting cheese so it's perfect for this delicious quick sandwich.

Serves
1

Temperature
370°F

Cooking Time
10 minutes

2 slices raisin bread

2 tablespoons butter, softened

2 teaspoons honey mustard

3 slices thinly sliced honey ham
(about 3 ounces)

4 slices Muenster cheese
(about 3 ounces)

2 toothpicks

1. Pre-heat the air fryer to 370ºF.

2. Spread the softened butter on one side of both slices of raisin bread and place the bread, buttered side down on the counter. Spread the honey mustard on the other side of each slice of bread. Layer 2 slices of cheese, the ham and the remaining 2 slices of cheese on one slice of bread and top with the other slice of bread. Remember to leave the buttered side of the bread on the outside.

3. Transfer the sandwich to the air fryer basket and secure the sandwich with toothpicks.

4. Air-fry at 370ºF for 5 minutes. Flip the sandwich over, remove the toothpicks and air-fry for another 5 minutes. Cut the sandwich in half and enjoy!!

 Substitution

Here's your basic grilled cheese sandwich! The variations of this sandwich are endless and up to you. Try sliced turkey and Swiss cheese, or Cheddar cheese and apple.

Arancini with Sun-dried Tomatoes and Mozzarella

This is super easy to do if you have leftover risotto. Otherwise, you'll have the step of cooking the Arborio rice before you can make the arancini, but you can do that step ahead of time, making last minute prep a breeze.

Serves
6

Temperature
380°F

Cooking Time
30 minutes
(15 minutes per batch)

1 tablespoon olive oil

½ small onion, finely chopped

1 cup Arborio rice

¼ cup white wine or dry vermouth

1 cup vegetable or chicken stock

1½ cups water

1 teaspoon salt

freshly ground black pepper

⅓ cup grated Parmigiano-Reggiano cheese

2 to 3 ounces mozzarella cheese

2 eggs, lightly beaten

¼ cup chopped oil-packed sun-dried tomatoes

1½ cups Italian seasoned breadcrumbs, divided

olive oil

marinara sauce, for serving

1. Start by cooking the Arborio rice.

    a. Stovetop Method: Pre-heat a medium saucepan over medium heat. Add the olive oil and sauté the onion until it starts to become tender – about 5 minutes. Add the rice and stir well to coat all the grains of rice. Add the white wine or vermouth. Let this simmer and get absorbed by the rice. Then add the stock and water, cover, reduce the heat to low and simmer for 20 minutes.

    b. Pressure-Cooker Method: Pre-heat the pressure cooker using the BROWN setting. Add the oil and cook the onion for a few minutes. Add the rice, wine, stock, water, salt and freshly ground black pepper, give everything one good stir and lock the lid in place. Pressure cook on HIGH for 7 minutes. Reduce the pressure with the QUICK-RELEASE method and carefully remove the lid.

    Taste the rice to make sure it is tender. Season with salt and freshly ground black pepper and stir in the grated Parmigiano-Reggiano cheese. Spread the rice out onto a baking sheet to cool.

2. While the rice is cooling, cut the mozzarella into ¾-inch cubes.

3. Once the rice has cooled, combine the rice with the eggs, sun-dried tomatoes and ½ cup of the breadcrumbs. Place the remaining breadcrumbs in a shallow dish. Shape the rice mixture into 12 balls. Press a hole in the rice ball with your finger and push one or two cubes of mozzarella cheese into the hole. Mold the rice back into a ball, enclosing the cheese. Roll the finished rice balls in the breadcrumbs and place them on a baking sheet while you make the remaining rice balls. Spray or brush the rice balls with olive oil.

4. Pre-heat the air fryer to 380°F.

5. Cook 6 arancini at a time. Air-fry for 10 minutes. Gently turn the arancini over, brush or spray with oil again and air-fry for another 5 minutes. Serve warm with the marinara sauce.

Cheesy Pigs in a Blanket

These are a cocktail party classic and staple. They've been done a million times, but they're always the first hors d'oeuvre to disappear at a gathering. Here we've stuffed a little cheese inside to make them extra special. Depending on how the smoked sausages are packed, you may have leftovers – throw the plain sausages into the air fryer too and your gluten-free friends will thank you.

Serves
4 to 6

Temperature
350°F

Cooking Time
7 minutes

24 cocktail size smoked sausages

6 slices deli-sliced Cheddar cheese, each cut into 8 rectangular pieces

1 (8-ounce) tube refrigerated crescent roll dough

ketchup or mustard for dipping

1. Unroll the crescent roll dough into one large sheet. If your crescent roll dough has perforated seams, pinch or roll all the perforated seams together. Cut the large sheet of dough into 4 rectangles. Then cut each rectangle into 6 pieces by making one slice lengthwise in the middle and 2 slices horizontally. You should have 24 pieces of dough.

2. Make a deep slit lengthwise down the center of the cocktail sausage. Stuff two pieces of cheese into the slit in the sausage. Roll one piece of crescent dough around the stuffed cocktail sausage leaving the ends of the sausage exposed. Pinch the seam together. Repeat with the remaining sausages.

3. Pre-heat the air fryer to 350°F.

4. Air-fry in 2 batches, placing the sausages seam side down in the basket. Air-fry for 7 minutes. Serve hot with ketchup or your favorite mustard for dipping.

You can also make this recipe with regular sized hot dogs, cutting the crescent roll to fit and wrapping it around the wiener. It's an easy weekday dinner that will put a smile on your kids' faces.

Warm Spinach Dip with Pita Chips

Making your own pita chips in your air fryer is easy and offers you the chance to control the flavor and use less oil. Get creative with your own homemade chips by trying different seasonings on them.

Serves
6 to 8

Temperature
390°F

Cooking Time
10 + 30 minutes

Pita Chips:

4 pita breads

1 tablespoon olive oil

½ teaspoon paprika

salt and freshly ground black pepper

Spinach Dip:

8 ounces cream cheese, softened at room temperature

1 cup ricotta cheese

1 cup grated Fontina cheese

½ teaspoon Italian seasoning

½ teaspoon garlic powder

¾ teaspoon salt

freshly ground black pepper

16 ounces frozen chopped spinach, thawed and squeezed dry

¼ cup grated Parmesan cheese

½ tomato, finely diced

¼ teaspoon dried oregano

1. Pre-heat the air fryer to 390°F.

2. Split the pita breads open so you have 2 circles. Cut each circle into 8 wedges. Place all the wedges into a large bowl and toss with the olive oil. Season with the paprika, salt and pepper and toss to coat evenly. Air-fry the pita triangles in two batches for 5 minutes each, shaking the basket once or twice while they cook so they brown and crisp evenly.

3. Combine the cream cheese, ricotta cheese, Fontina cheese, Italian seasoning, garlic powder, salt and pepper in a large bowl. Fold in the spinach and mix well.

4. Transfer the spinach-cheese mixture to a 7-inch ceramic baking dish or cake pan. Sprinkle the Parmesan cheese on top and wrap the dish with aluminum foil. Transfer the dish to the basket of the air fryer, lowering the dish into the basket using a sling made of aluminum foil (fold a piece of aluminum foil into a strip about 2-inches wide by 24-inches long). Fold the ends of the aluminum foil over the top of the dish before returning the basket to the air fryer. Air-fry for 30 minutes at 390°F. With 4 minutes left on the air fryer timer, remove the foil and let the cheese brown on top.

5. Sprinkle the diced tomato and oregano on the warm dip and serve immediately with the pita chips.

Did You Know...?

You can be ahead of the game with this appetizer! Prepare the dip, cover with the aluminum foil and refrigerate it overnight. Just remember to remove it from the refrigerator and let it sit on the countertop to come to room temperature for an hour before you cook it.

Crab Rangoon Dip with Wonton Chips

This chip and dip dish will be the hit of the party! The hardest part about this recipe is keeping the nibbling hands (including your own) off the wonton chips before the dip is done!

Serves
6 to 10

Temperature
370°F

Cooking Time
10 + 16 minutes

Wonton Chips:

1 (12-ounce) package wonton wrappers

vegetable oil

sea salt

Crab Rangoon Dip:

8 ounces cream cheese, softened

¾ cup sour cream

1 teaspoon Worcestershire sauce

1½ teaspoons soy sauce

1 teaspoon sesame oil

⅛ teaspoon ground cayenne pepper

¼ teaspoon salt

freshly ground black pepper

8 ounces cooked crabmeat

1 cup grated white Cheddar cheese

⅓ cup chopped scallions

paprika (for garnish)

1. Cut the wonton wrappers in half diagonally to form triangles. Working in batches, lay the wonton triangles on a flat surface and brush or spray both sides with vegetable oil.

2. Pre-heat the air fryer to 370ºF.

3. Place about 10 to 12 wonton triangles in the air fryer basket, letting them overlap slightly. Air-fry for just 2 minutes, shaking the basket halfway through the cooking time. Transfer the wonton chips to a large bowl and season immediately with sea salt. (You'll hear the chips start to spin around in the air fryer when they are almost done.) Repeat with the rest of wontons (keeping those fishing hands at bay!).

4. To make the dip, combine the cream cheese, sour cream, Worcestershire sauce, soy sauce, sesame oil, cayenne pepper, salt, and freshly ground black pepper in a bowl. Mix well and then fold in the crabmeat, Cheddar cheese, and scallions.

5. Transfer the dip to a 7-inch ceramic baking pan or shallow casserole dish. Sprinkle paprika on top and cover the dish with aluminum foil. Lower the dish into the air fryer basket using a sling made of aluminum foil (fold a piece of aluminum foil into a strip about 2-inches wide by 24-inches long). Air-fry for 11 minutes. Remove the aluminum foil and air-fry for another 5 minutes to finish cooking and brown the top. Serve hot with the wonton chips.

Did You Know...?

While jumbo lump crabmeat is delicious, it's expensive. In this recipe, the crabmeat falls apart in the dip, so less expensive regular lump crabmeat is perfect.

Spiced Nuts

These make a great snack or nibble for when guests arrive at your house. A bowl of these will disappear in no time, so make several batches and store them in an airtight container.

Makes
3 cups

Temperature
300ºF

Cooking Time
25 minutes

BJC FAV

1 egg white, lightly beaten

¼ cup sugar

1 teaspoon salt

½ teaspoon ground cinnamon

¼ teaspoon ground cloves

¼ teaspoon ground allspice

pinch ground cayenne pepper

1 cup pecan halves

1 cup cashews

1 cup almonds

1. Combine the egg white with the sugar and spices in a bowl.

2. Pre-heat the air fryer to 300ºF.

3. Spray or brush the air fryer basket with vegetable oil. Toss the nuts together in the spiced egg white and transfer the nuts to the air fryer basket.

4. Air-fry for 25 minutes, stirring the nuts in the basket a few times during the cooking process. Taste the nuts (carefully because they will be very hot) to see if they are crunchy and nicely toasted. Air-fry for a few more minutes if necessary.

5. Serve warm or cool to room temperature and store in an airtight container for up to two weeks.

BLUE JEAN Chef *Did You Know...?*

Nuts are high in oils, and consequently can turn rancid from exposure to light and heat. They can also take on the flavors of other things around them. So, the best way to store nuts is in airtight glass or plastic containers in the freezer.

See photo on page 22.

Pork Pot Stickers with Yum Yum Sauce

Everyone loves a pot sticker! This is another recipe that you can vary with different ingredients – substitute chicken or turkey for the pork, or omit the meat altogether and go vegetarian. The Yum Yum sauce is also very versatile. It's delicious not only with pot stickers, but with French fries, chicken fingers or even crudité.

Makes
48

Temperature
400°F

Cooking Time
24 minutes
(8 minutes per batch)

1 pound ground pork

2 cups shredded green cabbage

¼ cup shredded carrot

½ cup finely chopped water chestnuts

2 teaspoons minced fresh ginger

¼ cup hoisin sauce

2 tablespoons soy sauce

1 tablespoon sesame oil

freshly ground black pepper

3 scallions, minced

48 round dumpling wrappers (or wonton wrappers with the corners cut off to make them round)

1 tablespoon vegetable oil

soy sauce, for serving

Yum Yum Sauce:

1½ cups mayonnaise

2 tablespoons sugar

3 tablespoons rice vinegar

1 teaspoon soy sauce

2 tablespoons ketchup

1½ teaspoons paprika

¼ teaspoon ground cayenne pepper

¼ teaspoon garlic powder

1. Pre-heat a large sauté pan over medium-high heat. Add the ground pork and brown for a few minutes. Remove the cooked pork to a bowl using a slotted spoon and discard the fat from the pan. Return the cooked pork to the sauté pan and add the cabbage, carrots and water chestnuts. Sauté for a minute and then add the fresh ginger, hoisin sauce, soy sauce, sesame oil, and freshly ground black pepper. Sauté for a few more minutes, just until cabbage and carrots are soft. Then stir in the scallions and transfer the pork filling to a bowl to cool.

2. Make the pot stickers in batches of 12. Place 12 dumpling wrappers on a flat surface. Brush a little water around the perimeter of the wrappers. Place a rounded teaspoon of the filling into the center of each wrapper. Fold the wrapper over the filling, bringing the edges together to form a half moon, sealing the edges shut. Brush a little more water on the top surface of the sealed edge of the pot sticker. Make pleats in the dough around the sealed edge by pinching the dough and folding the edge over on itself. You should have about 5 to 6 pleats in the dough. Repeat this three times until you have 48 pot stickers. Freeze the pot stickers for 2 hours (or as long as 3 weeks in an airtight container).

3. Pre-heat the air fryer to 400ºF.

4. Air-fry the pot stickers in batches of 16. Brush or spray the pot stickers with vegetable oil just before putting them in the air fryer basket. Air-fry for 8 minutes, turning the pot stickers once or twice during the cooking process.

5. While the pot stickers are cooking, combine all the ingredients for the Yum Yum sauce in a bowl. Serve the pot stickers warm with the Yum Yum sauce and soy sauce for dipping.

Did You Know...?

You can freeze these pot stickers when they are raw OR cooked. If they are frozen raw, add a minute or two to the cooking time. If they are frozen after they have been cooked, simply re-heat in the air fryer at 350ºF for 4 to 5 minutes.

Shrimp Egg Rolls

For so many folks, egg rolls are the best part of Chinese takeout! Now you can make them at home with less oil. You can even freeze them and cook them later, or re-heat them nicely in the air fryer. Check the Asian aisle of your grocery store for the duck sauce, or pick your favorite dipping sauce.

Makes
8

Temperature
370°F

Cooking Time
20 minutes
(10 minutes per batch)

1 tablespoon vegetable oil

½ head green or savoy cabbage, finely shredded

1 cup shredded carrots

1 cup canned bean sprouts, drained

1 tablespoon soy sauce

½ teaspoon sugar

1 teaspoon sesame oil

¼ cup hoisin sauce

freshly ground black pepper

1 pound cooked shrimp, diced

¼ cup scallions

8 egg roll wrappers

vegetable oil

duck sauce

1. Pre-heat a large sauté pan over medium-high heat. Add the oil and cook the cabbage, carrots and bean sprouts until they start to wilt – about 3 minutes. Add the soy sauce, sugar, sesame oil, hoisin sauce and black pepper. Sauté for a few more minutes. Stir in the shrimp and scallions and cook until the vegetables are just tender. Transfer the mixture to a colander in a bowl to cool. Press or squeeze out any excess water from the filling so that you don't end up with soggy egg rolls.

2. To make the egg rolls, place the egg roll wrappers on a flat surface with one of the points facing towards you so they look like diamonds. Dividing the filling evenly between the eight wrappers, spoon the mixture onto the center of the egg roll wrappers. Spread the filling across the center of the wrappers from the left corner to the right corner, but leave 2 inches from each corner empty. Brush the empty sides of the wrapper with a little water. Fold the bottom corner of the wrapper tightly up over the filling, trying to avoid making any air pockets. Fold the left corner in toward the center and then the right corner toward the center. It should now look like an envelope. Tightly roll the egg roll from the bottom to the top open corner. Press to seal the egg roll together, brushing with a little extra water if need be. Repeat this technique with all 8 egg rolls.

3. Pre-heat the air fryer to 370ºF.

4. Spray or brush all sides of the egg rolls with vegetable oil. Air-fry four egg rolls at a time for 10 minutes, turning them over halfway through the cooking time.

5. Serve hot with duck sauce or your favorite dipping sauce.

Smart Tip

Egg rolls that are usually deep fried in Chinese food restaurants have roughly 380 calories per roll. Air frying your egg rolls takes this down to 210 calories.

210 Calories – 3g Fat – (0.5g Sat. Fat) – 27g Carbohydrates
2g Fiber – 7g Sugar – 17g Protein

Blooming Onion

Whether you know it as Outback Steakhouse's Bloomin' Onion® or Lone Star Steakhouse's Texas Rose, yes you can make one at home in your air fryer!

Serves
4

Temperature
350°F

Cooking Time
25 minutes

1 large Vidalia onion, peeled

2 eggs

½ cup milk

1 cup flour

1 teaspoon salt

½ teaspoon freshly ground black pepper

¼ teaspoon ground cayenne pepper

½ teaspoon paprika

½ teaspoon garlic powder

Dipping Sauce:

½ cup mayonnaise

½ cup ketchup

1 teaspoon Worcestershire sauce

½ teaspoon ground cayenne pepper

½ teaspoon paprika

½ teaspoon onion powder

1. Cut off the top inch of the onion, leaving the root end of the onion intact. Place the now flat, stem end of the onion down on a cutting board with the root end facing up. Make 16 slices around the onion, starting with your knife tip ½-inch away from the root so that you never slice through the root. Begin by making slices at 12, 3, 6 and 9 o'clock around the onion. Then make three slices down the onion in between each of the original four slices. Turn the onion over, gently separate the onion petals, and remove the loose pieces of onion in the center.

2. Combine the eggs and milk in a bowl. In a second bowl, combine the flour, salt, black pepper, cayenne pepper, paprika, and garlic powder.

3. Pre-heat the air fryer to 350°F.

4. Place the onion cut side up into a third empty bowl. Sprinkle the flour mixture all over the onion to cover it and get in between the onion petals. Turn the onion over to carefully shake off the excess flour and then transfer the onion to the empty flour bowl, again cut side up.

5. Pour the egg mixture all over the onion to cover all the flour. Let it soak for a minute in the mixture. Carefully remove the onion, tipping it upside down to drain off any excess egg, and transfer it to the empty egg bowl, again cut side up.

6. Finally, sprinkle the flour mixture over the onion a second time, making sure the onion is well coated and all the petals have the seasoned flour mixture on them. Carefully turn the onion over, shake off any excess flour and transfer it to a plate or baking sheet. Spray the onion generously with vegetable oil.

7. Transfer the onion, cut side up to the air fryer basket and air-fry for 25 minutes. The onion petals will open more fully as it cooks, so spray with more vegetable oil at least twice during the cooking time.

8. While the onion is cooking, make the dipping sauce by combining all the dip ingredients and mixing well. Serve the Blooming Onion as soon as it comes out of the air fryer with dipping sauce on the side.

This onion, shared with four people, comes in around 488 calories per serving at your traditional steakhouse. In an air fryer, that calorie count comes down to 45 calories for just the onion, or 267 calories for the onion AND the dipping sauce.

Onion and Sauce
267 Calories – 21g Fat – (3g Sat. Fat) – 19g Carbohydrates
2g Fiber – 9g Sugar – 2g Protein

Onion alone
45 Calories – 0.4g Fat – (0g Sat. Fat) – 10g Carbohydrates
2g Fiber – 2g Sugar – 1g Protein

Zucchini Fries with Roasted Garlic Aïoli

These are a nice change from potato fries. Don't try to skip a step in the dredging process – you need all three steps in order for the breading to stick to the zucchini. Although it will be difficult, try to let them cool ever so slightly before digging in because they are vey hot inside when they come out of the fryer.

Serves
4

Temperature
400°F

Cooking Time
12 minutes

Roasted Garlic Aïoli:

1 teaspoon roasted garlic

½ cup mayonnaise

2 tablespoons olive oil

juice of ½ lemon

salt and pepper

Zucchini Fries:

½ cup flour

2 eggs, beaten

1 cup seasoned breadcrumbs

salt and pepper

1 large zucchini, cut into ½-inch sticks

olive oil in a spray bottle, can or mister

1. To make the aïoli, combine the roasted garlic, mayonnaise, olive oil and lemon juice in a bowl and whisk well. Season the aïoli with salt and pepper to taste.

2. Prepare the zucchini fries. Create a dredging station with three shallow dishes. Place the flour in the first shallow dish and season well with salt and freshly ground black pepper. Put the beaten eggs in the second shallow dish. In the third shallow dish, combine the breadcrumbs, salt and pepper. Dredge the zucchini sticks, coating with flour first, then dipping them into the eggs to coat, and finally tossing in breadcrumbs. Shake the dish with the breadcrumbs and pat the crumbs onto the zucchini sticks gently with your hands so they stick evenly.

3. Place the zucchini fries on a flat surface and let them sit at least 10 minutes before air-frying to let them dry out a little. Pre-heat the air fryer to 400°F.

4. Spray the zucchini sticks with olive oil, and place them into the air fryer basket. You can air-fry the zucchini in two layers, placing the second layer in the opposite direction to the first. Air-fry for 12 minutes turning and rotating the fries halfway through the cooking time. Spray with additional oil when you turn them over.

5. Serve zucchini fries warm with the roasted garlic aïoli.

Did You Know...?

The air fryer is a great way to roast garlic. See page 229 for instructions on how to do it.

Breads
and
Breakfast

Cheddar Cheese Biscuits

Now here's something that is hard to resist! No matter how many times I make them, I always have to have a bite while they are warm, moist and delicious straight out of the air fryer. Trust me, these biscuits will make you a very popular cook! To make these biscuits in the air fryer, you'll need a 7-inch cake pan, but it's well worth the investment and you'll use it for so many recipes.

Makes
8 biscuits

Temperature
380°F

Cooking Time
22 minutes

2⅓ cups self-rising flour

2 tablespoons sugar

½ cup butter (1 stick),
frozen for 15 minutes

½ cup grated Cheddar cheese,
plus more to melt on top

1⅓ cups buttermilk

1 cup all-purpose flour, for shaping

1 tablespoon butter, melted

1. Line a buttered 7-inch metal cake pan with parchment paper or a silicone liner.

2. Combine the flour and sugar in a large mixing bowl. Grate the butter into the flour. Add the grated cheese and stir to coat the cheese and butter with flour. Then add the buttermilk and stir just until you can no longer see streaks of flour. The dough should be quite wet.

3. Spread the all-purpose (not self-rising) flour out on a small cookie sheet. With a spoon, scoop 8 evenly sized balls of dough into the flour, making sure they don't touch each other. With floured hands, coat each dough ball with flour and toss them gently from hand to hand to shake off any excess flour. Place each floured dough ball into the prepared pan, right up next to the other. This will help the biscuits rise up, rather than spreading out.

4. Pre-heat the air fryer to 380°F.

5. Transfer the cake pan to the basket of the air fryer, lowering it into the basket using a sling made of aluminum foil (fold a piece of aluminum foil into a strip about 2-inches wide by 24-inches long). Let the ends of the aluminum foil sling hang across the cake pan before returning the basket to the air fryer.

6. Air-fry for 20 minutes. Check the biscuits a couple of times to make sure they are not getting too brown on top. If they are, re-arrange the aluminum foil strips to cover any brown parts. After 20 minutes, check the biscuits by inserting a toothpick into the center of the biscuits. It should come out clean. If it needs a little more time, continue to air-fry for a couple of extra minutes. Brush the tops of the biscuits with some melted butter and sprinkle a little more grated cheese on top if desired. Pop the basket back into the air fryer for another 2 minutes. Remove the cake pan from the air fryer using the aluminum sling. Let the biscuits cool for just a minute or two and then turn them out onto a plate and pull apart. Serve immediately.

Self-rising flour is made from soft wheat with a lower protein content and produces a very tender biscuit. If you don't have any self-rising flour, you can use 2⅓ cups all purpose flour + 3½ teaspoons baking powder + ½ teaspoon salt instead.

Cinnamon Rolls
with Cream Cheese Glaze

Make these easy cinnamon rolls and your guests will think you spent all day in the kitchen! They are gooey and delicious and easily better than any cinnamon rolls you can buy, plus they'll give you bragging rights. 😊

Serves
8

Temperature
350°F

Cooking Time
18 minutes
(9 minutes per batch)

1 pound frozen bread dough, thawed

¼ cup butter, melted and cooled

¾ cup brown sugar

1½ tablespoons ground cinnamon

Cream Cheese Glaze:

4 ounces cream cheese, softened

2 tablespoons butter, softened

1¼ cups powdered sugar

½ teaspoon vanilla

1. Let the bread dough come to room temperature on the counter. On a lightly floured surface roll the dough into a 13-inch by 11-inch rectangle. Position the rectangle so the 13-inch side is facing you. Brush the melted butter all over the dough, leaving a 1-inch border uncovered along the edge farthest away from you.

2. Combine the brown sugar and cinnamon in a small bowl. Sprinkle the mixture evenly over the buttered dough, keeping the 1-inch border uncovered. Roll the dough into a log starting with the edge closest to you. Roll the dough tightly, making sure to roll evenly and push out any air pockets. When you get to the uncovered edge of the dough, press the dough onto the roll to seal it together.

3. Cut the log into 8 pieces slicing slowly with a sawing motion so you don't flatten the dough. Turn the slices on their sides and cover with a clean kitchen towel. Let the rolls sit in the warmest part of your kitchen for 1½ to 2 hours to rise.

4. To make the glaze, place the cream cheese and butter in a microwave-safe bowl. Soften the mixture in the microwave for 30 seconds at a time until it is easy to stir. Gradually add the powdered sugar and stir to combine. Add the vanilla extract and whisk until smooth. Set aside.

5. When the rolls have risen, pre-heat the air fryer to 350°F.

6. Transfer 4 of the rolls to the air fryer basket. Air-fry for 5 minutes. Turn the rolls over and air-fry for another 4 minutes. Repeat with the remaining 4 rolls.

7. Let the rolls cool for a couple of minutes before glazing. Spread large dollops of cream cheese glaze on top of the warm cinnamon rolls, allowing some of the glaze to drip down the side of the rolls. Serve warm and enjoy!

Did You Know...?

If you want to serve the rolls warm all at once, don't glaze the first batch right away. After air-frying the second batch of rolls, place the first batch back into the air fryer at 300°F for 1 minute. Once you've finished glazing the second batch, the first batch will be warm and ready to be glazed.

Hashbrown Potatoes Lyonnaise

This is a much tidier way of making fried potatoes for breakfast in the morning. Cooking in the air fryer keeps everything contained so there is no splatter anywhere. These simple and tasty potatoes should not be limited to breakfast, however. They are delicious any time of the day!

Serves
4

Temperature
370°F/400°F

Cooking Time
8 + 25 minutes

1 Vidalia (or other sweet) onion, sliced

1 teaspoon butter, melted

1 teaspoon brown sugar

2 large russet potatoes (about 1 pound), sliced ½-inch thick

1 tablespoon vegetable oil

salt and freshly ground black pepper

1. Pre-heat the air fryer to 370°F.

2. Toss the sliced onions, melted butter and brown sugar together in the air fryer basket. Air-fry for 8 minutes, shaking the basket occasionally to help the onions cook evenly.

3. While the onions are cooking, bring a 3-quart saucepan of salted water to a boil on the stovetop. Par-cook the potatoes in boiling water for 3 minutes. Drain the potatoes and pat them dry with a clean kitchen towel.

4. Add the potatoes to the onions in the air fryer basket and drizzle with vegetable oil. Toss to coat the potatoes with the oil and season with salt and freshly ground black pepper.

5. Increase the air fryer temperature to 400°F and air-fry for 20 to 25 minutes tossing the vegetables a few times during the cooking time to help the potatoes brown evenly. Season to taste again with salt and freshly ground black pepper and serve warm.

 Shortcut

You can skip the step of par-cooking the potatoes if you like, but you'll need to add 3 to 5 minutes to the final cooking time. Boiling the potatoes first gives you potatoes that are crispy on the outside, but tender and moist on the inside. Without the boiling, the potatoes will be less tender, but you'll save a few minutes.

See additional photo on page 62.

Roasted Vegetable Frittata

A frittata is simply a crust-less quiche or open-faced omelet. As with any quiche or omelet, you can add whatever you like to a frittata, so feel free to vary this recipe to your taste. Just make sure whatever ingredients you decide to add are cooked before you add them to the egg mixture.

Serves
1 to 2

Temperature
400°F/380°F

Cooking Time
6 + 13 minutes

½ red or green bell pepper, cut into ½-inch chunks

4 button mushrooms, sliced

½ cup diced zucchini

½ teaspoon chopped fresh oregano or thyme

1 teaspoon olive oil

3 eggs, beaten

¼ cup grated Cheddar cheese

salt and freshly ground black pepper, to taste

1 teaspoon butter

1 teaspoon chopped fresh parsley

1. Pre-heat the air fryer to 400°F.

2. Toss the peppers, mushrooms, zucchini and oregano with the olive oil and air-fry for 6 minutes, shaking the basket once or twice during the cooking process to redistribute the ingredients.

3. While the vegetables are cooking, beat the eggs well in a bowl, stir in the Cheddar cheese and season with salt and freshly ground black pepper. Add the air-fried vegetables to this bowl when they have finished cooking.

4. Place a 6- or 7-inch non-stick metal cake pan into the air fryer basket with the butter using an aluminum sling to lower the pan into the basket. (Fold a piece of aluminum foil into a strip about 2-inches wide by 24-inches long.) Air-fry for 1 minute at 380°F to melt the butter. Remove the cake pan and rotate the pan to distribute the butter and grease the pan. Pour the egg mixture into the cake pan and return the pan to the air fryer, using the aluminum sling.

5. Air-fry at 380°F for 12 minutes, or until the frittata has puffed up and is lightly browned. Let the frittata sit in the air fryer for 5 minutes to cool to an edible temperature and set up. Remove the cake pan from the air fryer, sprinkle with parsley and serve immediately.

The word "frittata" is Italian and roughly translates into "fried".

See additional photo on page 62.

Western Frittata

Here's your classic Western omelet in an Italian frittata style. You can substitute ingredients to your taste. Swap the ham out for bacon or sausage, or add broccoli instead of the bell pepper. You can even change the cheese you use. Make this your frittata!

Serves
1 to 2

Temperature
400°F/380°F

Cooking Time
6 + 13 minutes

½ red or green bell pepper, cut into ½-inch chunks

1 teaspoon olive oil

3 eggs, beaten

¼ cup grated Cheddar cheese

¼ cup diced cooked ham

salt and freshly ground black pepper, to taste

1 teaspoon butter

1 teaspoon chopped fresh parsley

1. Pre-heat the air fryer to 400°F.

2. Toss the peppers with the olive oil and air-fry for 6 minutes, shaking the basket once or twice during the cooking process to redistribute the ingredients.

3. While the vegetables are cooking, beat the eggs well in a bowl, stir in the Cheddar cheese and ham, and season with salt and freshly ground black pepper. Add the air-fried peppers to this bowl when they have finished cooking.

4. Place a 6- or 7-inch non-stick metal cake pan into the air fryer basket with the butter using an aluminum sling to lower the pan into the basket. (Fold a piece of aluminum foil into a strip about 2-inches wide by 24-inches long.) Air-fry for 1 minute at 380°F to melt the butter. Remove the cake pan and rotate the pan to distribute the butter and grease the pan. Pour the egg mixture into the cake pan and return the pan to the air fryer, using the aluminum sling.

5. Air-fry at 380°F for 12 minutes, or until the frittata has puffed up and is lightly browned. Let the frittata sit in the air fryer for 5 minutes to cool to an edible temperature and set up. Remove the cake pan from the air fryer, sprinkle with parsley and serve immediately.

 Substitution

Make this Italian frittata a little more Italian in taste by using prosciutto instead of the ham, roasted red peppers instead of the bell pepper, and some goat cheese or Fontina cheese instead of the Cheddar.

Roasted Tomato and Cheddar Rolls

This recipe takes a little time, so be prepared. The good news is that you can always start it a day ahead of time and finish it off quickly the next day. Remember... good things come to those who wait.

Makes
12 rolls

Temperature
390°F/330°F/360°F

Cooking Time
15 + 40 minutes
(10 minutes per batch)

4 Roma tomatoes

½ clove garlic, minced

1 tablespoon olive oil

¼ teaspoon dried thyme

salt and freshly ground black pepper

4 cups all-purpose flour

1 teaspoon active dry yeast

2 teaspoons sugar

2 teaspoons salt

1 tablespoon olive oil

1 cup grated Cheddar cheese,
plus more for sprinkling at the end

1½ cups water

1. Cut the Roma tomatoes in half, remove the seeds with your fingers and transfer to a bowl. Add the garlic, olive oil, dried thyme, salt and freshly ground black pepper and toss well.

2. Pre-heat the air fryer to 390°F.

3. Place the tomatoes, cut side up in the air fryer basket and air-fry for 10 minutes. The tomatoes should just start to brown. Shake the basket to redistribute the tomatoes, and air-fry for another 5 to10 minutes at 330°F until the tomatoes are no longer juicy. Let the tomatoes cool and then rough chop them.

4. Combine the flour, yeast, sugar and salt in the bowl of a stand mixer. Add the olive oil, chopped roasted tomatoes and Cheddar cheese to the flour mixture and start to mix using the dough hook attachment. As you're mixing, add 1¼ cups of the water, mixing until the dough comes together. Continue to knead the dough with the dough hook for another 10 minutes, adding enough water to the dough to get it to the right consistency.

5. Transfer the dough to an oiled bowl, cover with a clean kitchen towel and let it rest and rise until it has doubled in volume – about 1 to 2 hours. Then, divide the dough into 12 equal portions. Roll each portion of dough into a ball. Lightly coat each dough ball with oil and let the dough balls rest and rise a second time, covered lightly with plastic wrap for 45 minutes. (Alternately, you can place the rolls in the refrigerator overnight and take them out 2 hours before you bake them.)

6. Pre-heat the air fryer to 360°F.

7. Spray the dough balls and the air fryer basket with a little olive oil. Place three rolls at a time in the basket and bake for 10 minutes. Add a little grated Cheddar cheese on top of the rolls for the last 2 minutes of air frying for an attractive finish.

If you want to save a little time, or if it is not tomato season, you can substitute 1 cup of sun-dried tomatoes instead of roasting the tomatoes yourself.

Bacon Puff Pastry Pinwheels

This recipe doesn't qualify as "Super Easy" just because you do have to work with puff pastry, but it is very easy to put together. It's great for a weekend family breakfast or perfect for a brunch appetizer or brunch buffet.

Makes
8 pinwheels

Temperature
360°F

Cooking Time
10 minutes

1 sheet of puff pastry

2 tablespoons maple syrup

¼ cup brown sugar

8 slices bacon (not thick cut)

coarsely cracked black pepper

vegetable oil

1. On a lightly floured surface, roll the puff pastry out into a square that measures roughly 10 inches wide by however long your bacon strips are (usually about 11 inches). Cut the pastry into eight even strips.

2. Brush the strips of pastry with the maple syrup and sprinkle the brown sugar on top, leaving 1 inch of dough exposed at the far end of each strip. Place a slice of bacon on each strip of puff pastry, letting 1/8-inch of the length of bacon hang over the edge of the pastry. Season generously with coarsely ground black pepper.

3. With the exposed end of the pastry strips away from you, roll the bacon and pastry strips up into pinwheels. Dab a little water on the exposed end of the pastry and pinch it to the pinwheel to seal the pastry shut.

4. Pre-heat the air fryer to 360°F.

5. Brush or spray the air fryer basket with a little vegetable oil. Place the pinwheels into the basket and air-fry at 360°F for 8 minutes. Turn the pinwheels over and air-fry for another 2 minutes to brown the bottom. Serve warm.

 Dress It Up

If you're serving this for a brunch buffet, cut both the bacon slices and the puff pastry strips in half so they are only 5 inches or so long, and roll smaller pinwheels. You will have to cook these in batches, but you'll end up with 16 pinwheels instead of 8.

Soft Pretzels

You can make these pretzels any size you like and tie them any way you like too! They should be eaten on the same day they are made – ideally while they are still warm and buttery.

Makes
12 large, **24** medium or
48 mini prezels

Temperature
350°F

Cooking Time
6 minutes per batch

2 teaspoons yeast

1 cup water, warm

1 teaspoon sugar

1 teaspoon salt

2½ cups all-purpose flour

2 tablespoons butter, melted

1 cup boiling water

1 tablespoon baking soda

coarse sea salt

melted butter

1. Combine the yeast and water in a small bowl. Combine the sugar, salt and flour in the bowl of a stand mixer. With the mixer running and using the dough hook, drizzle in the yeast mixture and melted butter and knead dough until smooth and elastic – about 10 minutes. Shape into a ball and let the dough rise for 1 hour.

2. Punch the dough down to release any air and decide what size pretzels you want to make.

    a. To make large pretzels, divide the dough into 12 portions.

    b. To make medium sized pretzels, divide the dough into 24 portions.

    c. To make mini pretzel knots, divide the dough into 48 portions.

Roll each portion into a skinny rope using both hands on the counter and rolling from the center to the ends of the rope. Spin the rope into a pretzel shape (or tie the rope into a knot) and place the tied pretzels on a parchment lined baking sheet.

3. Pre-heat the air fryer to 350°F.

4. Combine the boiling water and baking soda in a shallow bowl and whisk to dissolve (this mixture will bubble, but it will settle down). Let the water cool so that you can put your hands in it. Working in batches, dip the pretzels (top side down) into the baking soda-water mixture and let them soak for 30 seconds to a minute. (This step is what gives pretzels their texture and helps them to brown faster.) Then, remove the pretzels carefully and return them (top side up) to the baking sheet. Sprinkle the coarse salt on the top.

6. Air-fry in batches for 3 minutes per side. When the pretzels are finished, brush them generously with the melted butter and enjoy them warm with some spicy mustard.

The average pretzel from a fast-food chain contains 340 calories, but these homemade pretzels come in around 115 calories. That's almost three for the price of one!

120 Calories – 2g Fat – (1.5g Sat. Fat)
20g Carbohydrates – 1g Fiber – 0g Sugar
3g Protein

Seasoned Herbed Sourdough Croutons

These are far superior to store bought croutons and a great way to use up leftover bread. Plus, you can make just as much as you need for any particular dish. Just remember to make a few extra because you'll be snacking on one or five while you make the rest of dinner!

Makes
4 cups

Temperature
400°F

Cooking Time
5 to 7 minutes

4 cups cubed sourdough bread,
1-inch cubes (about 8 ounces)

1 tablespoon olive oil

1 teaspoon fresh thyme leaves

¼ - ½ teaspoon salt

freshly ground black pepper

1. Combine all ingredients in a bowl and taste to make sure it is seasoned to your liking.

2. Pre-heat the air fryer to 400ºF.

3. Toss the bread cubes into the air fryer and air-fry for 5 to 7 minutes, shaking the basket once or twice while they cook.

4. Serve warm or store in an airtight container.

Substitution

You can use all kinds of bread for croutons – multi-grain, brioche, challah, baguette, or ciabatta – but different breads take different amounts of time to cook. So, just check the croutons when you shake the basket during the cooking process.

Crunchy French Toast Sticks

A crunchy cinnamon cereal is perfect for coating the French toast sticks, but you can really use any cereal you like. Crunchy French Toast Sticks are a tasty and fun breakfast, with or without the maple syrup (but I like it with!).

Serves
2 to 4

Temperature
400°F

Cooking Time
9 minutes

2 eggs, beaten

¾ cup milk

½ teaspoon vanilla extract

½ teaspoon ground cinnamon

1½ cups crushed crunchy cinnamon cereal, or any cereal flakes

4 slices Texas Toast
(or other bread that you can slice into 1-inch thick slices)

maple syrup, for serving

vegetable oil or melted butter

1. Combine the eggs, milk, vanilla and cinnamon in a shallow bowl. Place the crushed cereal in a second shallow bowl.

2. Trim the crusts off the slices of bread and cut each slice into 3 sticks. Dip the sticks of bread into the egg mixture, turning them over to coat all sides. Let the bread sticks absorb the egg mixture for ten seconds or so, but don't let them get too wet. Roll the bread sticks in the cereal crumbs, pressing the cereal gently onto all sides so that it adheres to the bread.

3. Pre-heat the air fryer to 400°F.

4. Spray or brush the air fryer basket with oil or melted butter. Place the coated sticks in the basket. It's ok to stack a few on top of the others in the opposite direction.

5. Air-fry for 9 minutes. Turn the sticks over a couple of times during the cooking process so that the sticks crisp evenly. Serve warm with the maple syrup or some berries.

Did You Know...?

Texas Toast, as with all things Texas, is bigger than regular sandwich bread. The slices are at least 1-inch thick and the bread itself is dense enough to absorb the egg custard and still hold it's shape. If you can't find Texas Toast in your grocery store, buy a dense loaf of sandwich bread that you can slice yourself. If it's a couple of days old, even better!

Bacon, Broccoli and Swiss Cheese Bread Pudding

Bread puddings are not always for dessert. This savory bread pudding is perfect for breakfast or brunch. Make this the night before, leave it in the refrigerator overnight and it will be ready to cook in the morning.

Serves
2 to 4

Temperature
400°F/330°F

Cooking Time
6 + 2 + 40 minutes

½ pound thick cut bacon,
cut into ¼-inch pieces

3 cups brioche bread or rolls,
cut into ½-inch cubes

3 eggs

1 cup milk

½ teaspoon salt

freshly ground black pepper

1 cup frozen broccoli florets,
thawed and chopped

1½ cups grated Swiss cheese

1. Pre-heat the air fryer to 400°F.

2. Air-fry the bacon for 6 to 10 minutes until crispy, shaking the basket a few times while it cooks to help it cook evenly. Remove the bacon and set it aside on a paper towel.

3. Air-fry the brioche bread cubes for 2 minutes to dry and toast lightly. (If your brioche is a few days old and slightly stale, you can omit this step.)

4. Butter a 6- or 7-inch cake pan. Combine all the ingredients in a large bowl and toss well. Transfer the mixture to the buttered cake pan, cover with aluminum foil and refrigerate the bread pudding overnight, or for at least 8 hours.

5. Remove the casserole from the refrigerator an hour before you plan to cook, and let it sit on the countertop to come to room temperature.

6. Pre-heat the air fryer to 330°F. Transfer the covered cake pan, to the basket of the air fryer, lowering the dish into the basket using a sling made of aluminum foil (fold a piece of aluminum foil into a strip about 2-inches wide by 24-inches long). Fold the ends of the aluminum foil over the top of the dish before returning the basket to the air fryer. Air-fry for 20 minutes. Remove the foil and air-fry for an additional 20 minutes. If the top starts to brown a little too much before the custard has set, simply return the foil to the pan. The bread pudding has cooked through when a skewer inserted into the center comes out clean.

Brioche is an egg-based bread similar to Challah. You can use any bread, however, for this bread pudding. Bread that is stale is helpful because it will absorb more of the custard.

Garlic Bread Knots

These little garlic bread knots are made so easily because they call for store-bought refrigerated dough. Make them whatever size you like – a big knot for a dinner roll, or smaller knots for a tasty little snack.

Serves
8

Temperature
350°F

Cooking Time
10 minutes
(5 minutes per batch)

¼ cup melted butter

2 teaspoons garlic powder

1 teaspoon dried parsley

1 (11-ounce) tube of refrigerated French bread dough

1. Mix the melted butter, garlic powder and dried parsley in a small bowl and set it aside.

2. To make smaller knots, cut the long tube of bread dough into 16 slices. If you want to make bigger knots, slice the dough into 8 slices. Shape each slice into a long rope about 6 inches long by rolling it on a flat surface with the palm of your hands. Tie each rope into a knot and place them on a plate.

3. Pre-heat the air fryer to 350°F.

4. Transfer half of the bread knots into the air fryer basket, leaving space in between each knot. Brush each knot with the butter mixture using a pastry brush.

5. Air-fry for 5 minutes. Remove the baked knots and brush a little more of the garlic butter mixture on each. Repeat with the remaining bread knots and serve warm.

Pepperoni Pizza Bread

This pizza bread makes a statement! It's easy to make, but so impressive to look at that everyone will be talking about it. It's fun to pull apart and eat too. Perfect for noshing on movie or game night!

Serves
4 to 6

Temperature
320°F

Cooking Time
13 to 15 minutes

7-inch round bread boule

2 cups grated mozzarella cheese

1 tablespoon dried oregano

1 cup pizza sauce

1 cup mini pepperoni or pepperoni slices, cut in quarters

Pizza sauce for dipping (optional)

1. Make 7 to 8 deep slices across the bread boule, leaving 1 inch of bread uncut at the bottom of every slice before you reach the cutting board. The slices should go about three quarters of the way through the boule and be about 2 inches apart from each other. Turn the bread boule 90 degrees and make 7 to 8 similar slices perpendicular to the first slices to form squares in the bread. Again, make sure you don't cut all the way through the bread.

2. Combine the mozzarella cheese and oregano in a small bowl.

3. Fill the slices in the bread with pizza sauce by gently spreading the bread apart and spooning the sauce in between the squares of bread. Top the sauce with the mozzarella cheese mixture and then the pepperoni. Do your very best to get the cheese and pepperoni in between the slices, rather than on top of the bread. Keep spreading the bread apart and stuffing the ingredients in, but be careful not to tear the bottom of the bread.

4. Pre-heat the air fryer to 320°F.

5. Transfer the bread boule to the air fryer basket and air-fry for 13 to 15 minutes, making sure the top doesn't get too dark. (It will just be the cheese on top that gets dark, so if you've done a good job of tucking the cheese in between the slices, this shouldn't be an issue.)

6. Carefully remove the bread from the basket with a spatula. Transfer it to a serving platter with more sauce to dip into if desired. Serve with a lot of napkins so that people can just pull the bread apart with their hands and enjoy!

The key to this recipe is to make sure you buy a round loaf that will fit into your air fryer. If you can't find a 7-inch round bread boule, this recipe will work with an oblong loaf of bread too. You'll just have to cut the ends off to fit the bread in the basket. It won't be quite as pretty, but will still be as delicious.

Ham and Cheddar Gritters

What do you get if you make a fritter out of grits? Well, a Gritter of course! If you're a lover of traditional grits, please don't let me dissuade you from using them by calling for quick-cooking grits in this recipe! I love traditional grits, but for the sake of time and convenience, I've used the quick-cooking variety for this fritter recipe.

Serves
6 to 8

Temperature
400°F

Cooking Time
36 minutes
(12 minutes per batch)

4 cups water

1 cup quick-cooking grits

¼ teaspoon salt

2 tablespoons butter

2 cups grated Cheddar cheese, divided

1 cup finely diced ham

1 tablespoon chopped chives

salt and freshly ground black pepper

1 egg, beaten

2 cups panko breadcrumbs

vegetable oil

1. Bring the water to a boil in a saucepan. Whisk in the grits and ¼ teaspoon of salt, and cook for 7 minutes until the grits are soft. Remove the pan from the heat and stir in the butter and 1 cup of the grated Cheddar cheese. Transfer the grits to a bowl and let them cool for just 10 to 15 minutes.

2. Stir the ham, chives and the rest of the cheese into the grits and season with salt and pepper to taste. Add the beaten egg and refrigerate the mixture for 30 minutes. (Try not to chill the grits much longer than 30 minutes, or the mixture will be too firm to shape into patties.)

3. While the grit mixture is chilling, make the country gravy and set it aside. (See recipe below.)

4. Place the panko breadcrumbs in a shallow dish. Measure out ¼-cup portions of the grits mixture and shape them into patties. Coat all sides of the patties with the panko breadcrumbs, patting them with your hands so the crumbs adhere to the patties. You should have about 16 patties. Spray both sides of the patties with oil.

5. Pre-heat the air fryer to 400ºF.

6. In batches of 5 or 6, air-fry the fritters for 8 minutes. Using a flat spatula, flip the fritters over and air-fry for another 4 minutes.

7. Serve hot with country gravy.

Country Gravy

Makes
2½ cups

¼ pound pork sausage, casings removed

1 tablespoon butter

2 tablespoons flour

2 cups whole milk

½ teaspoon salt

freshly ground black pepper

1 teaspoon fresh thyme leaves

1. Pre-heat a saucepan over medium heat. Add and brown the sausage, crumbling it into small pieces as it cooks. Add the butter and flour, stirring well to combine. Continue to cook for 2 minutes, stirring constantly.

2. Slowly pour in the milk, whisking as you do, and bring the mixture to a boil to thicken. Season with salt and freshly ground black pepper, lower the heat and simmer until the sauce has thickened to your desired consistency – about 3 to 5 minutes. Stir in the fresh thyme, season to taste and serve hot.

All-in-One Breakfast Toast

This is a quick and easy breakfast, which provides a satisfying start to the day. The cooking time in this recipe gives you a soft-boiled egg consistency. If you want a harder yolk, just add a minute or two to the cook time. Most importantly, get yourself a nice artisan bread loaf that you slice yourself so you have a good thick piece of bread.

Serves
1

Temperature
400°F/380°F

Cooking Time
3 + 7 minutes

1 strip of bacon, diced

1 slice of 1-inch thick bread (such as Texas Toast or hand-sliced bread)

1 tablespoon softened butter (optional)

1 egg

salt and freshly ground black pepper

¼ cup grated Colby or Jack cheese

1. Pre-heat the air fryer to 400°F.

2. Air-fry the bacon for 3 minutes, shaking the basket once or twice while it cooks. Remove the bacon to a paper towel lined plate and set aside.

3. Use a sharp paring knife to score a large circle in the middle of the slice of bread, cutting halfway through, but not all the way through to the cutting board. Press down on the circle in the center of the bread slice to create an indentation. If using, spread the softened butter on the edges and in the hole of the bread.

4. Transfer the slice of bread, hole side up, to the air fryer basket. Crack the egg into the center of the bread, and season with salt and pepper.

5. Air-fry at 380°F for 5 minutes. Sprinkle the grated cheese around the edges of the bread leaving the center of the yolk uncovered, and top with the cooked bacon. Press the cheese and bacon into the bread lightly to help anchor it to the bread and prevent it from blowing around in the air fryer.

6. Air-fry for one or two more minutes (depending on how you like your egg cooked), just to melt the cheese and finish cooking the egg. Serve immediately.

You can also make "eggs in a basket" using a hollowed out bread roll instead of a slice of bread. The cooking time is the same and if you get rolls small enough, you could probably fit 2 or 3 in your air fryer at once. Try this with the Roasted Tomato and Cheddar Rolls on page 73.

Steaks
and
Burgers

Marinated Rib-Eye Steak
with Herb Roasted Mushrooms

Steak cooked in the air fryer is simply delicious! The high heat blowing around the confined space of the air fryer not only browns the meat nicely, but also cooks it quickly, keeping the steak juicy and moist. Pre-heat the air fryer for a quick 2 minutes and roughly ten minutes later you'll be enjoying dinner. You might never cook a steak on a grill again!

Serves
2

Temperature
400°F

Cooking Time
10 to 15 minutes

2 tablespoons Worcestershire sauce

¼ cup red wine

2 (8-ounce) boneless rib-eye steaks

coarsely ground black pepper

8 ounces baby bella (cremini) mushrooms, stems trimmed and caps halved

2 tablespoons olive oil

1 teaspoon dried parsley

1 teaspoon fresh thyme leaves

salt and freshly ground black pepper

chopped fresh chives or parsley

1. Combine the Worcestershire sauce and red wine in a shallow baking dish. Add the steaks to the marinade, pierce them several times with the tines of a fork or a meat tenderizer and season them generously with the coarsely ground black pepper. Flip the steaks over and pierce the other side in a similar fashion, seasoning again with the coarsely ground black pepper. Marinate the steaks for 2 hours.

2. Pre-heat the air fryer to 400°F.

3. Toss the mushrooms in a bowl with the olive oil, dried parsley, thyme, salt and freshly ground black pepper. Transfer the steaks from the marinade to the air fryer basket, season with salt and scatter the mushrooms on top.

4. Air-fry the steaks for 10 minutes for medium-rare, 12 minutes for medium, or 15 minutes for well-done, flipping the steaks once halfway through the cooking time.

5. Serve the steaks and mushrooms together with the chives or parsley sprinkled on top. A good steak sauce or some horseradish would be a nice accompaniment.

Horseradish sauce goes nicely with this steak. Mix together 2 tablespoons of sour cream with 1 tablespoon of fresh horseradish, 1 teaspoon of chopped fresh chives or parsley, a little salt and some freshly ground black pepper.

Pepper Steak

Pepper steak is a fun and colorful dish –a Chinese-American stir-fry with the flavors of soy, ginger and sesame. This recipe starts by marinating the meat to enhance the flavors, and then ends by turning the marinade into a sauce to keep everything moist and delicious.

Serves
4

Temperature
350°F

Cooking Time
30 minutes

2 tablespoons cornstarch

1 tablespoon sugar

¾ cup beef broth

¼ cup hoisin sauce

3 tablespoons soy sauce

1 teaspoon sesame oil

½ teaspoon freshly ground black pepper

1½ pounds boneless New York strip steaks, sliced into ½-inch strips

1 onion, sliced

3 small bell peppers, red, yellow and green, sliced

1. Whisk the cornstarch and sugar together in a large bowl to break up any lumps in the cornstarch. Add the beef broth and whisk until combined and smooth. Stir in the hoisin sauce, soy sauce, sesame oil and freshly ground black pepper. Add the beef, onion and peppers, and toss to coat. Marinate the beef and vegetables at room temperature for 30 minutes, stirring a few times to keep meat and vegetables coated.

2. Pre-heat the air fryer to 350°F.

3. Transfer the beef, onion, and peppers to the air fryer basket with tongs, reserving the marinade. Air-fry the beef and vegetables for 30 minutes, stirring well two or three times during the cooking process.

4. While the beef is air-frying, bring the reserved marinade to a simmer in a small saucepan over medium heat on the stovetop. Simmer for 5 minutes until the sauce thickens.

5. When the steak and vegetables have finished cooking, transfer them to a serving platter. Pour the hot sauce over the pepper steak and serve with white rice.

To make sure your pepper steak is as tender as can be, slice the steaks against the grain. To do this, look for the lines of muscle fibers that run along the steak, and run your knife perpendicular to these lines.

Asian Glazed Meatballs

The mushrooms in these meatballs help to keep the meatballs moist, as well as give them flavor. I love using the Thai sweet chili sauce as a glaze, but if you can't find that, try some honey or some hoisin sauce.

Serves
4 to 6

Temperature
380°F

Cooking Time
30 minutes
(10 minutes per batch)

---

1 large shallot, finely chopped

2 cloves garlic, minced

1 tablespoon grated fresh ginger

2 teaspoons fresh thyme, finely chopped

1½ cups brown mushrooms, very finely chopped (a food processor works well here)

2 tablespoons soy sauce

freshly ground black pepper

1 pound ground beef

½ pound ground pork

3 egg yolks

1 cup Thai sweet chili sauce (spring roll sauce)

¼ cup toasted sesame seeds

2 scallions, sliced

1. Combine the shallot, garlic, ginger, thyme, mushrooms, soy sauce, freshly ground black pepper, ground beef and pork, and egg yolks in a bowl and mix the ingredients together. Gently shape the mixture into 24 balls, about the size of a golf ball.

2. Pre-heat the air fryer to 380ºF.

3. Working in batches, air-fry the meatballs for 8 minutes, turning the meatballs over halfway through the cooking time. Drizzle some of the Thai sweet chili sauce on top of each meatball and return the basket to the air fryer, air-frying for another 2 minutes. Reserve the remaining Thai sweet chili sauce for serving.

4. As soon as the meatballs are done, sprinkle with toasted sesame seeds and transfer them to a serving platter. Scatter the scallions around and serve warm.

 *Shortcut*

These meatballs can be made very quickly in a food processor. Start by chopping the shallot, garlic, ginger, thyme and mushrooms together. Then, add the soy sauce, meats and egg and pulse the mixture together. Just don't over-process the mixture or you'll end up with tough meatballs.

Provolone Stuffed Meatballs

What's not to love about a meatball with a cheesy surprise inside? You can put these meatballs over pasta with a marinara sauce, or line them up in a hoagie roll with some fixings for a more casual meal.

Serves
4 to 6 (12 meatballs)

Temperature
380°F

Cooking Time
24 minutes
(12 minutes per batch)

1 tablespoon olive oil

1 small onion, very finely chopped

1 to 2 cloves garlic, minced

¾ pound ground beef

¾ pound ground pork

¾ cup breadcrumbs

¼ cup grated Parmesan cheese

¼ cup finely chopped fresh parsley
(or 1 tablespoon dried parsley)

½ teaspoon dried oregano

1½ teaspoons salt

freshly ground black pepper

2 eggs, lightly beaten

5 ounces sharp or aged provolone cheese,
cut into 1-inch cubes

1. Pre-heat a skillet over medium-high heat. Add the oil and cook the onion and garlic until tender, but not browned.

2. Transfer the onion and garlic to a large bowl and add the beef, pork, breadcrumbs, Parmesan cheese, parsley, oregano, salt, pepper and eggs. Mix well until all the ingredients are combined. Divide the mixture into 12 evenly sized balls. Make one meatball at a time, by pressing a hole in the meatball mixture with your finger and pushing a piece of provolone cheese into the hole. Mold the meat back into a ball, enclosing the cheese.

3. Pre-heat the air fryer to 380ºF.

4. Working in two batches, transfer six of the meatballs to the air fryer basket and air-fry for 12 minutes, shaking the basket and turning the meatballs a couple of times during the cooking process. Repeat with the remaining six meatballs. You can pop the first batch of meatballs into the air fryer for the last two minutes of cooking to re-heat them. Serve warm.

 Substitution

Provolone cheese is ideal for this recipe because it is a good melting cheese, but it can be very mild in flavor. Ideally you should look for a sharp or aged provolone, but, if you can't find aged provolone, try using an Asiago or even pepper jack cheese for a little kick.

Carne Asada

Carne Asada translates into "beef grilled", so I guess we're cheating a little here by using an air fryer, but once you taste it you won't mind the inaccuracy. Carne Asada, which is traditionally skirt or flank steak that is sliced after it is cooked, can be served in so many ways. My favorite way is to serve it with tortillas, guacamole and a fresh salsa.

Serves
4

Temperature
390°F

Cooking Time
15 minutes

4 cloves garlic, minced

3 chipotle peppers in adobo, chopped

⅓ cup chopped fresh parsley

⅓ cup chopped fresh oregano

1 teaspoon ground cumin seed

juice of 2 limes

⅓ cup olive oil

1 to 1½ pounds flank steak
(depending on your appetites)

salt

tortillas and guacamole
(optional – for serving)

1. Make the marinade: Combine the garlic, chipotle, parsley, oregano, cumin, lime juice and olive oil in a non-reactive bowl. Coat the flank steak with the marinade and let it marinate for 30 minutes to 8 hours. (Don't leave the steak out of refrigeration for longer than 2 hours, however.)

2. Pre-heat the air fryer to 390ºF.

3. Remove the steak from the marinade and place it in the air fryer basket. Season the steak with salt and air-fry for 15 minutes, turning the steak over halfway through the cooking time and seasoning again with salt. This should cook the steak to medium. Add or subtract two minutes for medium-well or medium-rare.

4. Remember to let the steak rest before slicing the meat against the grain. Serve with warm tortillas, guacamole and a fresh salsa like the Tomato-Corn Salsa below.

Tomato-Corn Salsa

1 ear fresh corn kernels (about 1 cup)

1 cup chopped fresh tomato

¼ cup minced red onion,
rinsed with cool water

2 tablespoons chopped fresh cilantro

1 tablespoon olive oil

½ lime juiced

¼ teaspoon salt

freshly ground black pepper

1. Combine all the ingredients in a bowl. Set aside for 15 minutes and then serve.

See photo on page 88.

Zesty London Broil

London broil usually refers not to a cut of meat, but to a method of preparing it. So, while sometimes you'll see meat labeled "London Broil" in the supermarket, you're actually looking for round or flank steak for this dish. In order to make this dish truly London broil, be sure to marinate the steak overnight for the most tender and flavorful result.

Serves
4 to 6

Temperature
400°F

Cooking Time
20 to 28 minutes

⅔ cup ketchup

¼ cup honey

¼ cup olive oil

2 tablespoons apple cider vinegar

2 tablespoons Worcestershire sauce

2 tablespoons minced onion

½ teaspoon paprika

1 teaspoon salt

1 teaspoon freshly ground black pepper

2 pounds London broil, top round or flank steak (about 1-inch thick)

1. Combine the ketchup, honey, olive oil, apple cider vinegar, Worcestershire sauce, minced onion, paprika, salt and pepper in a small bowl and whisk together.

2. Generously pierce both sides of the meat with a fork or meat tenderizer and place it in a shallow dish. Pour the marinade mixture over the steak, making sure all sides of the meat get coated with the marinade. Cover and refrigerate overnight.

3. Pre-heat the air fryer to 400°F.

4. Transfer the London broil to the air fryer basket and air-fry for 20 to 28 minutes, depending on how rare or well done you like your steak. Flip the steak over halfway through the cooking time.

5. Remove the London broil from the air fryer and let it rest for five minutes on a cutting board. To serve, thinly slice the meat against the grain and transfer to a serving platter.

 Dress It Up

If you'd like a sauce to pour over the London broil, reserve the marinade and simmer it in a saucepan while the steak is air-frying.

Bacon Wrapped Filets Mignons

This is possibly the simplest way to dress up little filets mignons. The filet mignon is the most tender cut of beef, but not the most flavorful. Wrapping bacon around the steak is a classic technique to give it a little extra flavor.

Serves
4

Temperature
400°F

Cooking Time
18 minutes

4 slices bacon (not thick cut)

4 (8-ounce) filets mignons

1 tablespoon fresh thyme leaves

salt and freshly ground black pepper

1. Pre-heat the air fryer to 400°F.

2. Lay the bacon slices down on a cutting board and sprinkle the thyme leaves on the bacon slices. Remove any string tying the filets and place the steaks down on their sides on top of the bacon slices. Roll the bacon around the side of the filets and secure the bacon to the fillets with a toothpick or two.

3. Season the steaks generously with salt and freshly ground black pepper and transfer the steaks to the air fryer.

4. Air-fry for 18 minutes, turning the steaks over halfway through the cooking process. This should cook your steaks to about medium, depending on how thick they are. If you'd prefer your steaks medium-rare or medium-well, simply add or subtract two minutes from the cooking time. Remove the steaks from the air fryer and let them rest for 5 minutes before removing the toothpicks and serving. (Just enough time to quickly air-fry some vegetables to go with them!)

Dress It Up

Looking for an elegant sauce to pour over the filets mignons? Look no further. Well… just a little bit further. ☺

Easy Red Wine Butter Sauce

2 to 3 tablespoons butter, divided

1 tablespoon minced shallot

3 sprigs fresh thyme

1 cup red wine

salt and freshly ground black pepper

1. Pre-heat a skillet on the stovetop over medium-high heat. Add 1 tablespoon of butter and sauté the shallot and thyme for 3 to 4 minutes, or until the shallot starts to soften. Pour in the red wine and bring the mixture to a simmer. Reduce the heat and simmer the sauce until the liquid has reduced to ¼ cup.

2. Turn off the heat and stir in 1 or 2 tablespoons butter, until it tastes right to you. Remove the thyme sprigs, season to taste and pour over the cooked steaks.

Chicken Fried Steak with Gravy

Can't decide if you want fried chicken or steak... well here's your answer! Chicken fried steak is a little bit of both - a steak in chicken's clothing! Chicken fried steak is usually made with a cube steak, which is simply a top round or top sirloin steak that has been tenderized. Buying a cube steak will save you having to tenderize the steak yourself.

Serves
4

Temperature
400°F

Cooking Time
20 minutes
(10 minutes per batch)

½ cup flour

2 teaspoons salt, divided

freshly ground black pepper

¼ teaspoon garlic powder

1 cup buttermilk

1 cup fine breadcrumbs

4 tenderized top round steaks
(about 6 to 8 ounces each; ½-inch thick)

vegetable or canola oil

For the Gravy:

2 tablespoons butter or bacon drippings

¼ onion, minced (about ¼ cup)

1 clove garlic, smashed

¼ teaspoon dried thyme

3 tablespoons flour

1 cup milk

salt and lots of freshly ground
black pepper

a few dashes of Worcestershire sauce

Steak with Gravy
530 Calories – 19g Fat – 8g Sat. Fat
33g Carbohydrates – 3g Fiber – 6g Sugar – 52g Protein

Steak alone
410 Calories– 12g Fat – (3.5g Sat. Fat)
23g Carbohydrates – 2g Fiber – 2g Sugar – 49g Protein

1. Set up a dredging station. Combine the flour, 1 teaspoon of salt, black pepper and garlic powder in a shallow bowl. Pour the buttermilk into a second shallow bowl. Finally, put the breadcrumbs and 1 teaspoon of salt in a third shallow bowl.

2. Dip the tenderized steaks into the flour, then the buttermilk, and then the breadcrumb mixture, pressing the crumbs onto the steak. Place them on a baking sheet and spray both sides generously with vegetable or canola oil.

3. Pre-heat the air fryer to 400ºF.

4. Transfer the steaks to the air fryer basket, two at a time, and air-fry for 10 minutes, flipping the steaks over halfway through the cooking time. This will cook your steaks to medium. If you want the steaks cooked a little more or less, add or subtract a minute or two. Hold the first batch of steaks warm in a 170ºF oven while you cook the second batch.

5. While the steaks are cooking, make the gravy. Melt the butter in a small saucepan over medium heat on the stovetop. Add the onion, garlic and thyme and cook for five minutes, until the onion is soft and just starting to brown. Stir in the flour and cook for another five minutes, stirring regularly, until the mixture starts to brown. Whisk in the milk and bring the mixture to a boil to thicken. Season to taste with salt, lots of freshly ground black pepper and a few dashes of Worcestershire sauce.

6. Plate the chicken fried steaks with mashed potatoes and vegetables and serve the gravy at the table to pour over the top.

Smart Tip

Chicken Fried Steak out at your local diner can come in around 620 calories. By air-frying instead of pan- or deep-frying, you'll only be looking at 530 calories including the gravy!

Red Curry Flank Steak

Flank steak can be somewhat tough, so marinating it is the way to go to help tenderize it as well as add flavor. This recipe marinates the flank steak with red curry paste and other bright flavors. Serve this with some coconut rice and some air-fried spicy green beans (page 195) for a change of pace from the usual steak and potatoes.

Serves
4

Temperature
400°F

Cooking Time
12 to 18 minutes

3 tablespoons red curry paste

¼ cup olive oil

2 teaspoons grated fresh ginger

2 tablespoons soy sauce

2 tablespoons rice wine vinegar

3 scallions, minced

1½ pounds flank steak

fresh cilantro (or parsley) leaves

1. Mix the red curry paste, olive oil, ginger, soy sauce, rice vinegar and scallions together in a bowl. Place the flank steak in a shallow glass dish and pour half the marinade over the steak. Pierce the steak several times with a fork or meat tenderizer to let the marinade penetrate the meat. Turn the steak over, pour the remaining marinade over the top and pierce the steak several times again. Cover and marinate the steak in the refrigerator for 6 to 8 hours.

2. When you are ready to cook, remove the steak from the refrigerator and let it sit at room temperature for 30 minutes.

3. Pre-heat the air fryer to 400ºF.

4. Cut the flank steak in half so that it fits more easily into the air fryer and transfer both pieces to the air fryer basket. Pour the marinade over the steak. Air-fry for 12 to 18 minutes, depending on your preferred degree of doneness of the steak (12 minutes = medium rare). Flip the steak over halfway through the cooking time.

5. When your desired degree of doneness has been reached, remove the steak to a cutting board and let it rest for 5 minutes before slicing. Thinly slice the flank steak against the grain of the meat. Transfer the slices to a serving platter, pour any juice from the bottom of the air fryer over the sliced flank steak and sprinkle the fresh cilantro on top.

Curry paste is a blend of spices typically found in curry powder, but also includes additional ingredients like lemongrass, ginger, fresh chilies, galangal, and garlic to name a few. It also can include oil and vinegar, which help to transfer the flavors. Curry paste will keep indefinitely in the refrigerator, and you'll be surprised how often you can use it, so pick up a jar from the ethnic section of your grocery store.

Dijon Thyme Burgers

Here's a little French twist on a burger. It includes one of my favorite classic flavor combinations – Dijon mustard and thyme – and is served on a Brioche bun. This recipe makes 4 quarter-pounders, but if you want a bigger meal, just divide the meat mixture into three burgers.

Serves
3 to 4

Temperature
370°F/330°F

Cooking Time
18 minutes

1 pound lean ground beef

⅓ cup panko breadcrumbs

¼ cup finely chopped onion

3 tablespoons Dijon mustard

1 tablespoon chopped fresh thyme

4 teaspoons Worcestershire sauce

1 teaspoon salt

freshly ground black pepper

Topping (optional):

2 tablespoons Dijon mustard

1 tablespoon dark brown sugar

1 teaspoon Worcestershire sauce

4 ounces sliced Swiss cheese, optional

1. Combine all the burger ingredients together in a large bowl and mix well. Divide the meat into 4 equal portions and then form the burgers, being careful not to over-handle the meat. One good way to do this is to throw the meat back and forth from one hand to another, packing the meat each time you catch it. Flatten the balls into patties, making an indentation in the center of each patty with your thumb (this will help it stay flat as it cooks) and flattening the sides of the burgers so that they will fit nicely into the air fryer basket.

2. Pre-heat the air fryer to 370ºF.

3. If you don't have room for all four burgers, air-fry two or three burgers at a time for 8 minutes. Flip the burgers over and air-fry for another 6 minutes.

4. While the burgers are cooking combine the Dijon mustard, dark brown sugar, and Worcestershire sauce in a small bowl and mix well. This optional topping to the burgers really adds a boost of flavor at the end. Spread the Dijon topping evenly on each burger. If you cooked the burgers in batches, return the first batch to the cooker at this time – it's ok to place the fourth burger on top of the others in the center of the basket. Air-fry the burgers for another 3 minutes.

5. Finally, if desired, top each burger with a slice of Swiss cheese. Lower the air fryer temperature to 330ºF and air-fry for another minute to melt the cheese. Serve the burgers on toasted brioche buns, dressed the way you like them.

Did You Know...?

The timing of this recipe depends on how thick you make the burgers. If cooking four burgers at one time, this timing should give you burgers that are medium to medium-well. If you like your burgers a little less cooked, subtract a minute or two.

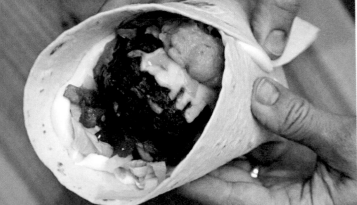

Mexican Cheeseburgers

This is what happens when you can't decide if you want a burger or a buritto. You mix it up and end up having both!

Serves
4

Temperature
370°F/340°F

Cooking Time
22 minutes

1¼ pounds ground beef

¼ cup finely chopped onion

½ cup crushed yellow corn tortilla chips

1 (1.25-ounce) packet taco seasoning

¼ cup canned diced green chilies

1 egg, lightly beaten

4 ounces pepper jack cheese, grated

4 (12-inch) flour tortillas

shredded lettuce, sour cream, guacamole, salsa (for topping)

1. Combine the ground beef, minced onion, crushed tortilla chips, taco seasoning, green chilies, and egg in a large bowl. Mix thoroughly until combined – your hands are good tools for this. Divide the meat into four equal portions and shape each portion into an oval-shaped burger.

2. Pre-heat the air fryer to 370°F.

3. Air-fry the burgers for 18 minutes, turning them over halfway through the cooking time. Divide the cheese between the burgers, lower fryer to 340°F and air-fry for an additional 4 minutes to melt the cheese. (This will give you a burger that is medium-well. If you prefer your cheeseburger medium-rare, shorten the cooking time to about 15 minutes and then add the cheese and proceed with the recipe.)

4. While the burgers are cooking, warm the tortillas wrapped in aluminum foil in a 350°F oven, or in a skillet with a little oil over medium-high heat for a couple of minutes. Keep the tortillas warm until the burgers are ready.

5. To assemble the burgers, spread sour cream over three quarters of the tortillas and top each with some shredded lettuce and salsa. Place the Mexican cheeseburgers on the lettuce and top with guacamole. Fold the tortillas around the burger, starting with the bottom and then folding the sides in over the top. (A little sour cream can help hold the seam of the tortilla together.) Serve immediately. Olé

Did You Know...?

You can also make these in the traditional burger shape and serve them on hamburger buns. As always, the toppings are completely up to you!

Inside Out Cheeseburgers

You'll never have to worry about the pickles and cheese sliding off your burger with this recipe, because they're stuffed inside the patty! Even the sauces – ketchup and mustard – are inside the patty, so you can save time building your burger and start sinking your teeth in sooner!

Serves
2

Temperature
370°F

Cooking Time
20 minutes

¾ pound lean ground beef

3 tablespoons minced onion

4 teaspoons ketchup

2 teaspoons yellow mustard

salt and freshly ground black pepper

4 slices of Cheddar cheese,
broken into smaller pieces

8 hamburger dill pickle chips

1. Combine the ground beef, minced onion, ketchup, mustard, salt and pepper in a large bowl. Mix well to thoroughly combine the ingredients. Divide the meat into four equal portions.

2. To make the stuffed burgers, flatten each portion of meat into a thin patty. Place 4 pickle chips and half of the cheese onto the center of two of the patties, leaving a rim around the edge of the patty exposed. Place the remaining two patties on top of the first and press the meat together firmly, sealing the edges tightly. With the burgers on a flat surface, press the sides of the burger with the palm of your hand to create a straight edge. This will help keep the stuffing inside the burger while it cooks.

3. Pre-heat the air fryer to 370ºF.

4. Place the burgers inside the air fryer basket and air-fry for 20 minutes, flipping the burgers over halfway through the cooking time.

5. Serve the cheeseburgers on buns with lettuce and tomato.

 Substitution

You can use this recipe to make different types of burgers. Instead of pickles and cheese, why not stuff it with onions, sautéed mushrooms and Swiss cheese? Or maybe blue cheese and bacon? The burger is your oyster! ☺

Pork
and
Lamb

Honey Mesquite Pork Chops

Mesquite is a type of tree, native to the southwestern United States and Mexico. When something has mesquite flavor, it has been grilled over burning mesquite wood. Assuming that you do not have any mesquite trees over which you can cook, here's a simple solution – just use mesquite seasoning, which you can find in most grocery stores. That makes this recipe super easy and the pork chop super tasty!

Serves
2

Temperature
330°F/400°F

Cooking Time
10 minutes

2 tablespoons mesquite seasoning

¼ cup honey

1 tablespoon olive oil

1 tablespoon water

freshly ground black pepper

2 bone-in center cut pork chops
(about 1 pound)

1.   Whisk the mesquite seasoning, honey, olive oil, water and freshly ground black pepper together in a shallow glass dish. Pierce the chops all over and on both sides with a fork or meat tenderizer. Add the pork chops to the marinade and massage the marinade into the chops. Cover and marinate for 30 minutes.

2.   Pre-heat the air fryer to 330ºF.

3.   Transfer the pork chops to the air fryer basket and pour half of the marinade over the chops, reserving the remaining marinade. Air-fry the pork chops for 6 minutes. Flip the pork chops over and pour the remaining marinade on top. Air-fry for an additional 3 minutes at 330ºF. Then, increase the air fryer temperature to 400ºF and air-fry the pork chops for an additional minute.

4.   Transfer the pork chops to a serving plate, and let them rest for 5 minutes before serving. If you'd like a sauce for these chops, pour the cooked marinade from the bottom of the air fryer over the top.

Substitution

You can cook bigger, thicker pork chops using this same recipe, but remember to increase the cooking time accordingly. Pork chops should cook to an internal temperature of 155ºF to 160ºF before resting for 5 minutes.

Spicy Hoisin BBQ Pork Chops

Hoisin sauce has a sweet and salty flavor – as do ketchup and BBQ sauce. So, it just makes sense that you can make a BBQ sauce with hoisin sauce as the main flavor component.

Serves
2 to 3

Temperature
400°F

Cooking Time
12 minutes

3 tablespoons hoisin sauce

¼ cup honey

1 tablespoon soy sauce

3 tablespoons rice vinegar

2 tablespoons brown sugar

1½ teaspoons grated fresh ginger

1 to 2 teaspoons Sriracha sauce, to taste

2 to 3 bone-in center cut pork chops,
1-inch thick (about 1¼ pounds)

chopped scallions, for garnish

1. Combine the hoisin sauce, honey, soy sauce, rice vinegar, brown sugar, ginger, and Sriracha sauce in a small saucepan. Whisk the ingredients together and bring the mixture to a boil over medium-high heat on the stovetop. Reduce the heat and simmer the sauce until it has reduced in volume and thickened slightly – about 10 minutes.

2. Pre-heat the air fryer to 400°F.

3. Place the pork chops into the air fryer basket and pour half the hoisin BBQ sauce over the top. Air-fry for 6 minutes. Then, flip the chops over, pour the remaining hoisin BBQ sauce on top and air-fry for 5 to 6 more minutes, depending on the thickness of the pork chops. The internal temperature of the pork chops should be 155°F when tested with an instant read thermometer.

4. Let the pork chops rest for 5 minutes before serving. You can spoon a little of the sauce from the bottom drawer of the air fryer over the top if desired. Sprinkle with chopped scallions and serve.

Sriracha sauce is a hot chili sauce, which originated in Thailand and has become very popular in the USA. You can find Sriracha sauce in the condiment section of your grocery store. It not only adds flavor, but packs some heat to your pork chops as well, so add it gradually.

Bacon, Blue Cheese and Pear Stuffed Pork Chops

This is a great recipe to vary and make your own. Change the stuffing by eliminating the bacon, adding dried cranberries or walnuts, or using a different cheese. It's a basic recipe that can turn into many different dinners.

Serves
3

Temperature
400°F/360°F

Cooking Time
6 + 18 minutes

4 slices bacon, chopped

1 tablespoon butter

½ cup finely diced onion

⅓ cup chicken stock

1½ cups seasoned stuffing cubes

1 egg, beaten

½ teaspoon dried thyme

½ teaspoon salt

⅛ teaspoon black pepper

1 pear, finely diced

⅓ cup crumbled blue cheese

3 boneless center-cut pork chops (2-inch thick)

olive oil

salt and freshly ground black pepper

1. Pre-heat the air fryer to 400°F.

2. Place the bacon into the air fryer basket and air-fry for 6 minutes, stirring halfway through the cooking time. Remove the bacon and set it aside on a paper towel. Pour out the grease from the bottom of the air fryer.

3. To make the stuffing, melt the butter in a medium saucepan over medium heat on the stovetop. Add the onion and sauté for a few minutes, until it starts to soften. Add the chicken stock and simmer for 1 minute. Remove the pan from the heat and add the stuffing cubes. Stir until the stock has been absorbed. Add the egg, dried thyme, salt and freshly ground black pepper, and stir until combined. Fold in the diced pear and crumbled blue cheese.

4. Place the pork chops on a cutting board. Using the palm of your hand to hold the chop flat and steady, slice into the side of the pork chop to make a pocket in the center of the chop. Leave about an inch of chop uncut and make sure you don't cut all the way through the pork chop. Brush both sides of the pork chops with olive oil and season with salt and freshly ground black pepper. Stuff each pork chop with a third of the stuffing, packing the stuffing tightly inside the pocket.

5. Preheat the air fryer to 360°F.

6. Spray or brush the sides of the air fryer basket with oil. Place the pork chops in the air fryer basket with the open stuffed edge of the pork chop facing the outside edges of the basket.

7. Air-fry the pork chops for 18 minutes, turning the pork chops over halfway through the cooking time. When the chops are done, let them rest for 5 minutes and then transfer to a serving platter.

Did You Know...?

Center-cut pork chops are usually rib chops or loin chops with the bone removed. They are very lean and tender, but have a relatively mild flavor. They are good for this recipe because we're stuffing them with bold flavors and without a bone, they fit more easily into the air fryer.

Apple Cornbread Stuffed Pork Loin
with Apple Gravy

Though this can be a tight fit in a smaller air fryer, you'll be amazed at how beautifully this stuffed pork loin turns out. The outside browns so nicely as you rotate the loin throughout the cooking process. Then, once sliced, it makes for such a pretty presentation that your guests will be very impressed with your skills.

Serves
4 to 6

Temperature
400°F/360°F

Cooking Time
6 + 55 minutes

4 strips of bacon, chopped

1 Granny Smith apple, peeled, cored and finely chopped

2 teaspoons fresh thyme leaves

¼ cup chopped fresh parsley

2 cups cubed cornbread

½ cup chicken stock

salt and freshly ground black pepper

1 (2-pound) boneless pork loin

kitchen twine

Apple Gravy:

2 tablespoons butter

1 shallot, minced

1 Granny Smith apple, peeled, cored and finely chopped

3 sprigs fresh thyme

2 tablespoons flour

1 cup chicken stock

½ cup apple cider

salt and freshly ground black pepper, to taste

1. Pre-heat the air fryer to 400ºF.

2. Add the bacon to the air fryer and air-fry for 6 to 8 minutes until crispy. While the bacon is cooking, combine the apple, fresh thyme, parsley and cornbread in a bowl and toss well. Moisten the mixture with the chicken stock and season to taste with salt and freshly ground black pepper. Add the cooked bacon to the mixture.

3. Butterfly the pork loin by holding it flat on the cutting board with one hand, while slicing into the pork loin parallel to the cutting board with the other. Slice into the longest side of the pork loin, but stop before you cut all the way through. You should then be able to open the pork loin up like a book, making it twice as wide as it was when you started. Season the inside of the pork with salt and freshly ground black pepper.

4. Spread the cornbread mixture onto the butterflied pork loin, leaving a one-inch border around the edge of the pork. Roll the pork loin up around the stuffing to enclose the stuffing, and tie the rolled pork in several places with kitchen twine or secure with toothpicks. Try to replace any stuffing that falls out of the roast as you roll it, by stuffing it into the ends of the rolled pork. Season the outside of the pork with salt and freshly ground black pepper.

5. Pre-heat the air fryer to 360ºF.

6. Place the stuffed pork loin into the air fryer, seam side down. Air-fry the pork loin for 15 minutes at 360ºF. Turn the pork loin over and air-fry for an additional 15 minutes. Turn the pork loin a quarter turn and air-fry for an additional 15 minutes. Turn the pork loin over again to expose the fourth side, and air-fry for an additional 10 minutes. The pork loin should register 155ºF on an instant read thermometer when it is finished.

7. While the pork is cooking, make the apple gravy. Pre-heat a saucepan over medium heat on the stovetop and melt the butter. Add the shallot, apple and thyme sprigs and sauté until the apple starts to soften and brown a little. Add the flour and stir for a minute or two. Whisk in the stock and apple cider vigorously to prevent the flour from forming lumps. Bring the mixture to a boil to thicken and season to taste with salt and pepper.

8. Transfer the pork loin to a resting plate and loosely tent with foil, letting the pork rest for at least 5 minutes before slicing and serving with the apple gravy poured over the top.

Pork Schnitzel with Dill Sauce

Schnitzel, originating in Austria, is a flattened piece of pork that is breaded and then fried. In this recipe, you lightly brush the breaded pork with a mixture of butter and oil. It gives the schnitzel delicious flavor, and you don't have to stand over a pan of bubbling oil.

Serves
4 to 6

Temperature
400°F

Cooking Time
24 minutes
(4 minutes per chop)

6 boneless, center cut pork chops (about 1½ pounds)

½ cup flour

1½ teaspoons salt

freshly ground black pepper

2 eggs

½ cup milk

1½ cups toasted fine breadcrumbs

1 teaspoon paprika

3 tablespoons butter, melted

2 tablespoons vegetable or olive oil

lemon wedges

Dill Sauce:

1 cup chicken stock

1½ tablespoons cornstarch

⅓ cup sour cream

1½ tablespoons chopped fresh dill

salt and pepper

1. Trim the excess fat from the pork chops and pound each chop with a meat mallet between two pieces of plastic wrap until they are ½-inch thick.

2. Set up a dredging station. Combine the flour, salt, and black pepper in a shallow dish. Whisk the eggs and milk together in a second shallow dish. Finally, combine the breadcrumbs and paprika in a third shallow dish.

3. Dip each flattened pork chop in the flour. Shake off the excess flour and dip each chop into the egg mixture. Finally dip them into the breadcrumbs and press the breadcrumbs onto the meat firmly. Place each finished chop on a baking sheet until they are all coated.

4. Pre-heat the air fryer to 400°F.

5. Combine the melted butter and the oil in a small bowl and lightly brush both sides of the coated pork chops. Do not brush the chops too heavily or the breading will not be as crispy.

6. Air-fry one schnitzel at a time for 4 minutes, turning it over halfway through the cooking time. Hold the cooked schnitzels warm on a baking pan in a 170°F oven while you finish air-frying the rest.

7. While the schnitzels are cooking, whisk the chicken stock and cornstarch together in a small saucepan over medium-high heat on the stovetop. Bring the mixture to a boil and simmer for 2 minutes. Remove the saucepan from heat and whisk in the sour cream. Add the chopped fresh dill and season with salt and pepper.

8. Transfer the pork schnitzel to a platter and serve with dill sauce and lemon wedges. For a traditional meal, serve this along side some egg noodles, spätzle or German potato salad.

 Smart Tip

Schnitzel is usually fried in a lot of oil, giving it a calorie count of around 690 calories. This schnitzel uses only a light brushed coating of butter and oil and has a calorie count of 370, or 414 including a little delicious dill sauce on top.

Pork and Sauce
414 Calories – 21g Fat – (9g Sat. Fat) – 24g Carbohydrates
1g Fiber – 3g Sugar – 30g Protein

Pork alone
370 Calories – 19g Fat – (7g Sat. Fat) – 20g Carbohydrates
1g Fiber – 2g Sugar – 29g Protein

See photo on page 108.

Mustard and Rosemary Pork Tenderloin with Fried Apples

Pork tenderloin is very easy to cook, but also very easy to over-cook. So, make sure you have your instant read thermometer at hand and check the pork as it approaches the finish line. It should read 155°F and then rest for 5 minutes while the apples cook.

Serves
2 to 3

Temperature
370°F/400°F

Cooking Time
18 + 8 minutes

1 pork tenderloin (about 1-pound)

2 tablespoons coarse brown mustard

salt and freshly ground black pepper

1½ teaspoons finely chopped fresh rosemary, plus sprigs for garnish

2 apples, cored and cut into 8 wedges

1 tablespoon butter, melted

1 teaspoon brown sugar

1. Pre-heat the air fryer to 370ºF.

2. Cut the pork tenderloin in half so that you have two pieces that fit into the air fryer basket. Brush the mustard onto both halves of the pork tenderloin and then season with salt, pepper and the fresh rosemary. Place the pork tenderloin halves into the air fryer basket and air-fry for 10 minutes. Turn the pork over and air-fry for an additional 5 to 8 minutes or until the internal temperature of the pork registers 155ºF on an instant read thermometer. If your pork tenderloin is especially thick, you may need to add a minute or two, but it's better to check the pork and add time, than to over-cook it.

3. Let the pork rest for 5 minutes. In the meantime, toss the apple wedges with the butter and brown sugar and air-fry at 400ºF for 8 minutes, shaking the basket once or twice during the cooking process so the apples cook and brown evenly.

4. Slice the pork on the bias. Serve with the fried apples scattered over the top and a few sprigs of rosemary as garnish.

Dress It Up

You can use this recipe to make a platter of hors d'oeuvres. Slice the pork and place it on a toasted crostini with a little goat cheese or a thin slice of Brie, a fried apple and a little fresh thyme or parsley.

Rack of Lamb with Pistachio Crust

A rack of lamb is always impressive and can be a very romantic meal too. This is perfect for date night!

Serves
2

Temperature
380°F

Cooking Time
19 minutes

½ cup finely chopped pistachios

3 tablespoons panko breadcrumbs

1 teaspoon chopped fresh rosemary

2 teaspoons chopped fresh oregano

salt and freshly ground black pepper

1 tablespoon olive oil

1 rack of lamb, bones trimmed of fat and frenched

1 tablespoon Dijon mustard

1. Pre-heat the air fryer to 380ºF.

2. Combine the pistachios, breadcrumbs, rosemary, oregano, salt and pepper in a small bowl. (This is a good job for your food processor if you have one.) Drizzle in the olive oil and stir to combine.

3. Season the rack of lamb with salt and pepper on all sides and transfer it to the air fryer basket with the fat side facing up. Air-fry the lamb for 12 minutes. Remove the lamb from the air fryer and brush the fat side of the lamb rack with the Dijon mustard. Coat the rack with the pistachio mixture, pressing the breadcrumbs onto the lamb with your hands and rolling the bottom of the rack in any of the crumbs that fall off.

4. Return the rack of lamb to the air fryer and air-fry for another 3 to 7 minutes or until an instant read thermometer reads 140°F for medium. Add or subtract a couple of minutes for lamb that is more or less well cooked. (Your time will vary depending on how big the rack of lamb is.)

5. Let the lamb rest for at least 5 minutes. Then, slice into chops and serve.

Did You Know...?

A "frenched" rack of lamb simply means one that has the rib bones exposed. You can usually find racks of lamb that have already been frenched at the supermarket, but if not ask the butcher to do it for you. You can do it yourself, but it does take a little time and practice.

Lamb Koftas
Meatballs

Koftas are meatballs of Middle Eastern origin. Delicious and easy to make, they are usually grilled on skewers but if you don't have skewers for your air fryer, you can cook them just as you would cook other meatballs. Traditionally, koftas are oval in shape, but you can shape them any way you like.

Serves
3 to 4

Temperature
400°F

Cooking Time
8 minutes

1 pound ground lamb

1 teaspoon ground cumin

1 teaspoon ground coriander

2 tablespoons chopped fresh mint

1 egg, beaten

½ teaspoon salt

freshly ground black pepper

1. Combine all ingredients in a bowl and mix together well. Divide the mixture into 10 portions. Roll each portion into a ball and then by cupping the meatball in your hand, shape it into an oval.

2. Pre-heat the air fryer to 400°F.

3. Air-fry the koftas for 8 minutes.

4. Serve warm with the cucumber-yogurt dip.

Cucumber-Yogurt Dip

½ English cucumber, grated (1 cup)

salt

½ clove garlic, finely minced

1 cup plain yogurt

1 tablespoon olive oil

1 tablespoon chopped fresh dill

freshly ground black pepper

1. Place the grated cucumber in a strainer and sprinkle with salt. Let this drain while the koftas are cooking. Meanwhile, combine the garlic, yogurt, oil and fresh dill in a bowl. Just before serving, stir the cucumber into the yogurt sauce and season to taste with freshly ground black pepper.

Lamb Burger with Feta and Olives

Here's a burger with a Greek flavor profile. If you like lamb, this is the burger for you! Looking for a cucumber sauce to go with it? Check out the previous page recipe for cucumber-yogurt dip.

Serves
3 to 4

Temperature
370°F

Cooking Time
16 minutes

2 teaspoons olive oil

⅓ onion, finely chopped

1 clove garlic, minced

1 pound ground lamb

2 tablespoons fresh parsley, finely chopped

1½ teaspoons fresh oregano, finely chopped

½ cup black olives, finely chopped

⅓ cup crumbled feta cheese

½ teaspoon salt

freshly ground black pepper

4 thick pita breads

toppings and condiments

1. Pre-heat a medium skillet over medium-high heat on the stovetop. Add the olive oil and cook the onion until tender, but not browned – about 4 to 5 minutes. Add the garlic and cook for another minute. Transfer the onion and garlic to a mixing bowl and add the ground lamb, parsley, oregano, olives, feta cheese, salt and pepper. Gently mix the ingredients together.

2. Divide the mixture into 3 or 4 equal portions and then form the hamburgers, being careful not to over-handle the meat. One good way to do this is to throw the meat back and forth between your hands like a baseball, packing the meat each time you catch it. Flatten the balls into patties, making an indentation in the center of each patty. Flatten the sides of the patties as well to make it easier to fit them into the air fryer basket.

3. Pre-heat the air fryer to 370ºF.

4. If you don't have room for all four burgers, air-fry two or three burgers at a time for 8 minutes at 370ºF. Flip the burgers over and air-fry for another 8 minutes. If you cooked your burgers in batches, return the first batch of burgers to the air fryer for the last two minutes of cooking to re-heat. This should give you a medium-well burger. If you'd prefer a medium-rare burger, shorten the cooking time to about 13 minutes. Remove the burgers to a resting plate and let the burgers rest for a few minutes before dressing and serving.

5. While the burgers are resting, toast the pita breads in the air fryer for 2 minutes. Tuck the burgers into the toasted pita breads, or wrap the pitas around the burgers and serve with a tzatziki sauce or some mayonnaise.

Substitution

Lamb has a strong flavor. If you want to lighten the flavor of this burger, just substitute ½ pound of ground beef for ½ pound of the ground lamb.

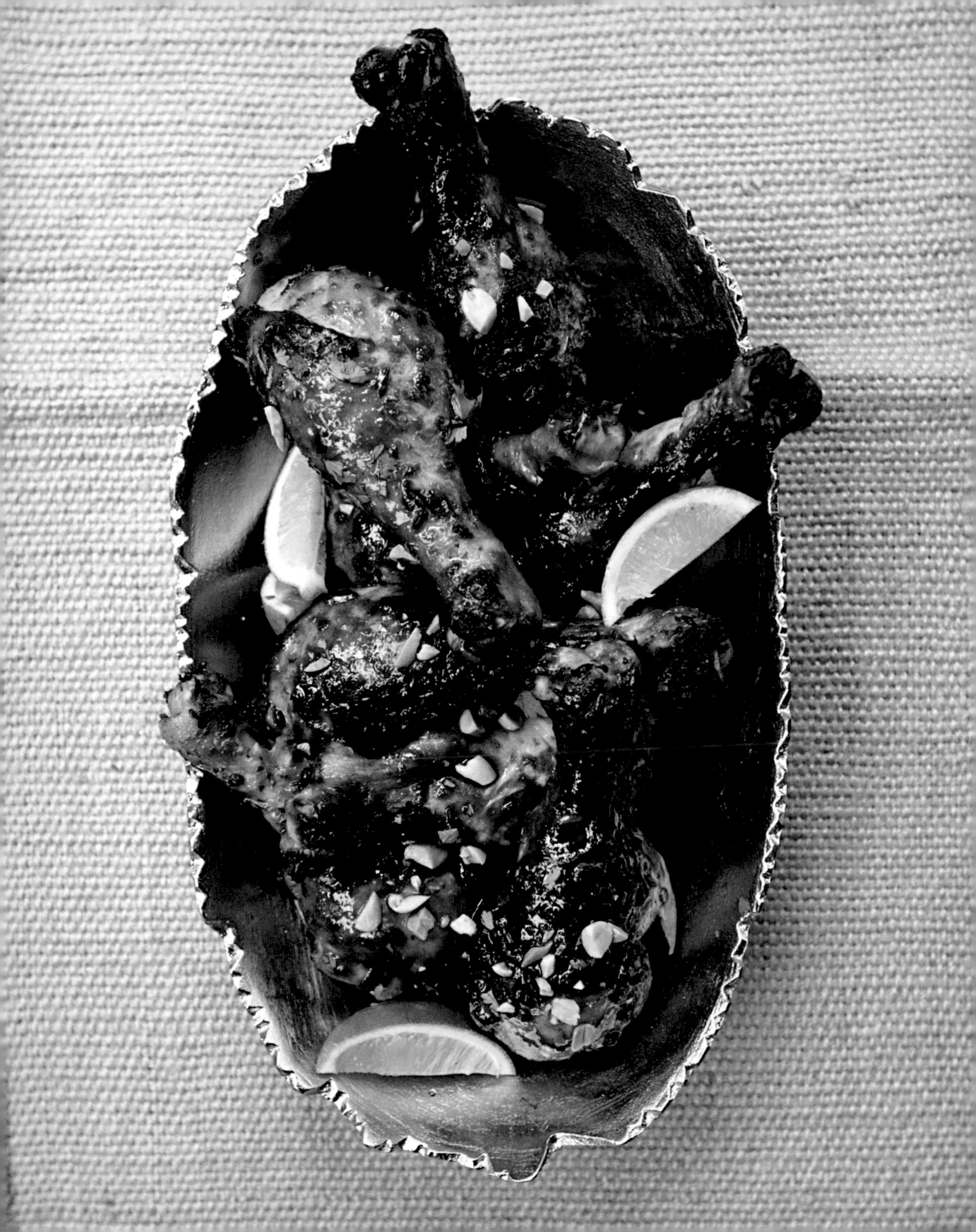

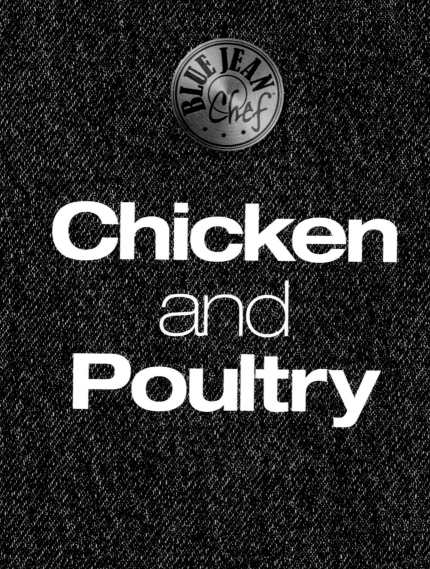

Chicken
and
Poultry

Honey Lemon Thyme Glazed Cornish Hen

A Cornish hen is not actually a game bird, but a young, small broiler chicken with very tender meat that takes flavors really well. If you can't find a Cornish hen, you can substitute bone-in chicken breasts in this recipe and it will still be delicious.

Serves
2

Temperature
390°F

Cooking Time
20 minutes

1 (2-pound) Cornish game hen, split in half

olive oil

salt and freshly ground black pepper

¼ teaspoon dried thyme

¼ cup honey

1 tablespoon lemon zest

juice of 1 lemon

1½ teaspoons chopped fresh thyme leaves

½ teaspoon soy sauce

freshly ground black pepper

1. Split the game hen in half by cutting down each side of the backbone and then cutting through the breast. Brush or spray both halves of the game hen with the olive oil and then season with the salt, pepper and dried thyme.

2. Pre-heat the air fryer to 390°F.

3. Place the game hen, skin side down, into the air fryer and air-fry for 5 minutes. Turn the hen halves over and air-fry for 10 minutes.

4. While the hen is cooking, combine the honey, lemon zest and juice, fresh thyme, soy sauce and pepper in a small bowl.

5. When the air fryer timer rings, brush the honey glaze onto the game hen and continue to air-fry for another 3 to 5 minutes, just until the hen is nicely glazed, browned and has an internal temperature of 165°F.

6. Let the hen rest for 5 minutes and serve warm.

Did You Know...?

It is much easier to zest a whole lemon than half a lemon. So, if a recipe calls for both zest and juice, remember to zest the lemon first and then slice it in half and juice it.

Crispy Duck with Cherry Sauce

You can make this recipe with a whole duck, cut in half, or you can use just duck breasts or just duck legs. It all depends on what you can find or what you're in the mood for.

Serves
2 to 4

Temperature
400°F

Cooking Time
33 minutes

1 whole duck (up to 5 pounds),
split in half, back and rib bones removed

1 teaspoon olive oil

salt and freshly ground black pepper

Cherry Sauce:

1 tablespoon butter

1 shallot, minced

½ cup sherry

¾ cup cherry preserves

1 cup chicken stock

1 teaspoon white wine vinegar

1 teaspoon fresh thyme leaves

salt and freshly ground black pepper

1. Pre-heat the air fryer to 400°F.

2. Trim some of the fat from the duck. Rub olive oil on the duck and season with salt and pepper. Place the duck halves in the air fryer basket, breast side up and facing the center of the basket.

3. Air-fry the duck for 20 minutes. Turn the duck over and air-fry for another 6 minutes.

4. While duck is air-frying, make the cherry sauce. Melt the butter in a large sauté pan. Add the shallot and sauté until it is just starting to brown – about 2 to 3 minutes. Add the sherry and deglaze the pan by scraping up any brown bits from the bottom of the pan. Simmer the liquid for a few minutes, until it has reduced by half. Add the cherry preserves, chicken stock and white wine vinegar. Whisk well to combine all the ingredients. Simmer the sauce until it thickens and coats the back of a spoon – about 5 to 7 minutes. Season with salt and pepper and stir in the fresh thyme leaves.

5. When the air fryer timer goes off, spoon some cherry sauce over the duck and continue to air-fry at 400°F for 4 more minutes. Then, turn the duck halves back over so that the breast side is facing up. Spoon more cherry sauce over the top of the duck, covering the skin completely. Air-fry for 3 more minutes and then remove the duck to a plate to rest for a few minutes.

6. Serve the duck in halves, or cut each piece in half again for a smaller serving. Spoon any additional sauce over the duck or serve it on the side.

 **Substitution**

If you're not particularly fond of duck, or can't find duck at your grocery store, this recipe can be easily adapted to Cornish game hen. Just change the cooking time to 5 minutes skin side down, 10 minutes skin side up and then spoon the sauce on and air-fry for another 5 minutes. Check out the Honey Lemon Thyme Glazed Cornish Game Hen recipe on page 124 for more guidance.

Sweet Chili Spiced Chicken

This is a favorite spice rub of mine that I use for chicken a lot. You might want to make a double or even triple batch and set some aside for future seasonings!

Serves
4

Temperature
370°F/340°F

Cooking Time
43 minutes
(20 minutes per batch + 3 minutes)

Spice Rub:

2 tablespoons brown sugar

2 tablespoons paprika

1 teaspoon dry mustard powder

1 teaspoon chili powder

2 tablespoons coarse sea salt
or kosher salt

2 teaspoons coarsely ground black pepper

1 tablespoon vegetable oil

1 (3½-pound) chicken, cut into 8 pieces

1. Prepare the spice rub by combining the brown sugar, paprika, mustard powder, chili powder, salt and pepper. Rub the oil all over the chicken pieces and then rub the spice mix onto the chicken, covering completely. This is done very easily in a zipper sealable bag. You can do this ahead of time and let the chicken marinate in the refrigerator, or just proceed with cooking right away.

2. Pre-heat the air fryer to 370°F.

3. Air-fry the chicken in two batches. Place the two chicken thighs and two drumsticks into the air fryer basket. Air-fry at 370°F for 10 minutes. Then, gently turn the chicken pieces over and air-fry for another 10 minutes. Remove the chicken pieces and let them rest on a plate while you cook the chicken breasts. Air-fry the chicken breasts, skin side down for 8 minutes. Turn the chicken breasts over and air-fry for another 12 minutes.

4. Lower the temperature of the air fryer to 340°F. Place the first batch of chicken on top of the second batch already in the basket and air-fry for a final 3 minutes.

5. Let the chicken rest for 5 minutes and serve warm with some mashed potatoes and a green salad or vegetables.

Tandoori Chicken Legs

Tandoori chicken is a very popular Indian chicken dish that is usually bright red from a highly spiced yogurt marinade (and sometimes some food coloring). It is traditionally prepared in a "tandoor" or a cylindrical clay oven. We've changed that to a cylindrical air fryer! Keep your eye on this one – it browns quickly.

Serves
2

Temperature
380°F

Cooking Time
30 minutes

1 cup plain yogurt

2 cloves garlic, minced

1 tablespoon grated fresh ginger

2 teaspoons paprika

2 teaspoons ground coriander

1 teaspoon ground turmeric

1 teaspoon salt

¼ teaspoon ground cayenne pepper

juice of 1 lime

2 bone-in, skin-on chicken legs

fresh cilantro leaves

1. Make the marinade by combining the yogurt, garlic, ginger, spices and lime juice. Make slashes into the chicken legs to help the marinade penetrate the meat. Pour the marinade over the chicken legs, cover and let the chicken marinate for at least an hour or overnight in the refrigerator.

2. Pre-heat the air fryer to 380°F.

3. Transfer the chicken legs from the marinade to the air fryer basket, reserving any extra marinade. Air-fry for 15 minutes. Flip the chicken over and pour the remaining marinade over the top. Air-fry for another 15 minutes, watching to make sure it doesn't brown too much. If it does start to get too brown, you can loosely tent the chicken with aluminum foil, tucking the ends of the foil under the chicken to stop it from blowing around.

4. Serve over rice with some fresh cilantro on top.

Substitution

You can easily substitute bone-in chicken breasts for the chicken legs in this recipe. The timing should be about the same, unless the chicken breasts you have are huge. If that's the case, increase the cooking time a little, but watch for that browning.

Pickle Brined Fried Chicken

This is a delicious fried chicken recipe that uses up the brine left in the pickle jar when you've finished all the pickles. This recipe calls for legs, but if you prefer white meat, feel free to substitute bone-in chicken breasts instead.

Serves
4

Temperature
370°F/340°F

Cooking Time
47 minutes
(20 minutes per batch + 7 minutes)

4 bone-in, skin-on chicken legs, cut into drumsticks and thighs (about 3½ pounds)

pickle juice from a 24-ounce jar of kosher dill pickles

½ cup flour

salt and freshly ground black pepper

2 eggs

1 cup fine breadcrumbs

1 teaspoon salt

1 teaspoon freshly ground black pepper

½ teaspoon ground paprika

⅛ teaspoon ground cayenne pepper

vegetable or canola oil in a spray bottle

1. Place the chicken in a shallow dish and pour the pickle juice over the top. Cover and transfer the chicken to the refrigerator to brine in the pickle juice for 3 to 8 hours.

2. When you are ready to cook, remove the chicken from the refrigerator to let it come to room temperature while you set up a dredging station. Place the flour in a shallow dish and season well with salt and freshly ground black pepper. Whisk the eggs in a second shallow dish. In a third shallow dish, combine the breadcrumbs, salt, pepper, paprika and cayenne pepper.

3. Pre-heat the air fryer to 370°F.

4. Remove the chicken from the pickle brine and gently dry it with a clean kitchen towel. Dredge each piece of chicken in the flour, then dip it into the egg mixture, and finally press it into the breadcrumb mixture to coat all sides of the chicken. Place the breaded chicken on a plate or baking sheet and spray each piece all over with vegetable oil.

5. Air-fry the chicken in two batches. Place two chicken thighs and two drumsticks into the air fryer basket. Air-fry for 10 minutes. Then, gently turn the chicken pieces over and air-fry for another 10 minutes. Remove the chicken pieces and let them rest on plate – do not cover. Repeat with the second batch of chicken, air-frying for 20 minutes, turning the chicken over halfway through.

6. Lower the temperature of the air fryer to 340°F. Place the first batch of chicken on top of the second batch already in the basket and air-fry for an additional 7 minutes. Serve warm and enjoy.

Smart Tip

Fried chicken usually comes along with 540 calories per serving. By air-frying this tasty chicken, we've brought that calorie count down to 376.

376 Calories – 21g Fat – (5g Sat. Fat)
25g Carbohydrates – 2g Fiber – 2g – Sugar21g Protein

Did You Know...?

If you don't have a jar of pickles on hand for this recipe, you can make your own quick pickle brine. Combine 1 cup of vinegar (white or cider), 1½ cups of water, 2 tablespoons of kosher salt (not iodized salt), 2 teaspoons of sugar, a couple of garlic cloves (thinly sliced) and roughly 2 tablespoons of a spice combination (dill seed, celery seed, coriander seed, mustard seed, black peppercorns) and bring to a boil. Cool completely before you pour the brine over the chicken.

Spinach and Feta Stuffed Chicken Breasts

This recipe can be a template for so many variations! Once you get the hang of creating the pocket in the chicken breast this will become a go-to dinner.

Serves
4

Temperature
380°F

Cooking Time
27 minutes
(12 minutes per batch + 3 minutes)

1 (10-ounce) package frozen spinach, thawed and drained well

1 cup feta cheese, crumbled

½ teaspoon freshly ground black pepper

4 boneless chicken breasts

salt and freshly ground black pepper

1 tablespoon olive oil

1. Prepare the filling. Squeeze out as much liquid as possible from the thawed spinach. Rough chop the spinach and transfer it to a mixing bowl with the feta cheese and the freshly ground black pepper.

2. Prepare the chicken breast. Place the chicken breast on a cutting board and press down on the chicken breast with one hand to keep it stabilized. Make an incision about 1-inch long in the fattest side of the breast. Move the knife up and down inside the chicken breast, without poking through either the top or the bottom, or the other side of the breast. The inside pocket should be about 3-inches long, but the opening should only be about 1-inch wide. If this is too difficult, you can make the incision longer, but you will have to be more careful when cooking the chicken breast since this will expose more of the stuffing.

3. Once you have prepared the chicken breasts, use your fingers to stuff the filling into each pocket, spreading the mixture down as far as you can.

4. Pre-heat the air fryer to 380°F.

5. Lightly brush or spray the air fryer basket and the chicken breasts with olive oil. Transfer two of the stuffed chicken breasts to the air fryer. Air-fry for 12 minutes, turning the chicken breasts over halfway through the cooking time. Remove the chicken to a resting plate and air-fry the second two breasts for 12 minutes. Return the first batch of chicken to the air fryer with the second batch and air-fry for 3 more minutes. When the chicken is cooked, an instant read thermometer should register 165°F in the thickest part of the chicken, as well as in the stuffing.

6. Remove the chicken breasts and let them rest on a cutting board for 2 to 3 minutes. Slice the chicken on the bias and serve with the slices fanned out.

You can stuff the chicken with endless combinations of ingredients. Try combining some chopped sun-dried tomatoes, ham and grated Swiss cheese for a twist on Chicken Cordon Bleu.

Jerk Chicken Drumsticks

You can make this wet spice rub and put it on any piece of chicken you like. If you prefer the breast meat, go ahead and rub this on bone-in chicken breasts and cook two at a time for 15 minutes per side.

Serves
2 to 3

Temperature
400°F

Cooking Time
20 minutes

1 or 2 cloves garlic

1 inch of fresh ginger

2 serrano peppers,
(with seeds if you like it spicy,
seeds removed for less heat)

1 teaspoon ground allspice

1 teaspoon ground nutmeg

1 teaspoon chili powder

½ teaspoon dried thyme

½ teaspoon ground cinnamon

½ teaspoon paprika

1 tablespoon brown sugar

1 teaspoon soy sauce

2 tablespoons vegetable oil

6 skinless chicken drumsticks

1. Combine all the ingredients except the chicken in a small chopper or blender and blend to a paste. Make slashes into the meat of the chicken drumsticks and rub the spice blend all over the chicken (a pair of plastic gloves makes this really easy). Transfer the rubbed chicken to a non-reactive covered container and let the chicken marinate for at least 30 minutes or overnight in the refrigerator.

2. Pre-heat the air fryer to 400°F.

3. Transfer the drumsticks to the air fryer basket. Air-fry for 10 minutes. Turn the drumsticks over and air-fry for another 10 minutes. Serve warm with some rice and vegetables or a green salad.

Did You Know...?

Many soy sauces do include gluten in their recipe, but it is possible to get gluten-free soy sauce. Tamari is a variety of soy sauce that is usually gluten-free, but you should always check the labels and look for the gluten-free stamp. If you find a gluten-free soy sauce, this recipe will be gluten-free too!

Philly Chicken Cheesesteak Stromboli

This was a special request from my good friend, David Venable. Though he's from North Carolina, he's adopted the Philadelphia chicken cheesesteak as one of his favorite sandwiches. Here it is in Stromboli form, just for him!

Serves
2 to 4

Temperature
400°F/370°F

Cooking Time
16 + 12 minutes

½ onion, sliced

1 teaspoon vegetable oil

2 boneless, skinless chicken breasts, partially frozen and sliced very thin on the bias (about 1 pound)

1 tablespoon Worcestershire sauce

salt and freshly ground black pepper

½ recipe of Blue Jean Chef pizza dough (see page 229), or 14 ounces of store-bought pizza dough

1½ cups grated Cheddar cheese

½ cup Cheese Whiz® (or other jarred cheese sauce), warmed gently in the microwave

tomato ketchup for serving

Substitution

In the mood for a traditional cheesesteak stromboli? Just substitute 1 pound of shaved beef for the chicken. If you can't find fresh shaved beef, use frozen steak sandwich meat, breaking it up a little before putting it into the air fryer basket and adding a minute or two to the cooking time.

1. Pre-heat the air fryer to 400°F.

2. Toss the sliced onion with oil and air-fry for 8 minutes, stirring halfway through the cooking time. Add the sliced chicken and Worcestershire sauce to the air fryer basket, and toss to evenly distribute the ingredients. Season the mixture with salt and freshly ground black pepper and air-fry for 8 minutes, stirring a couple of times during the cooking process. Remove the chicken and onion from the air fryer and let the mixture cool a little.

3. On a lightly floured surface, roll or press the pizza dough out into a 13-inch by 11-inch rectangle, with the long side closest to you. Sprinkle half of the Cheddar cheese over the dough leaving an empty 1-inch border from the edge farthest away from you. Top the cheese with the chicken and onion mixture, spreading it out evenly. Drizzle the cheese sauce over the meat and sprinkle the remaining Cheddar cheese on top.

4. Start rolling the stromboli away from you and toward the empty border. Make sure the filling stays tightly tucked inside the roll. Finally, tuck the ends of the dough in and pinch the seam shut. Place the seam side down and shape the Stromboli into a U-shape to fit in the air-fry basket (see page 170 Roasted Vegetable Stromboli on how to do this). Cut 4 small slits with the tip of a sharp knife evenly in the top of the dough and lightly brush the stromboli with a little oil.

5. Pre-heat the air fryer to 370°F.

6. Spray or brush the air fryer basket with oil and transfer the U-shaped stromboli to the air fryer basket. Air-fry for 12 minutes, turning the stromboli over halfway through the cooking time. (Use a plate to invert the stromboli out of the air fryer basket and then slide it back into the basket off the plate.)

7. To remove, carefully flip stromboli over onto a cutting board. Let it rest for a couple of minutes before serving. Slice the stromboli into 3-inch pieces and serve with ketchup for dipping, if desired.

Tortilla Crusted Chicken Breast

This recipe is like a Mexican style chicken Parmesan! It's super easy to make, but the fun part of this recipe is that you can change the flavor and appearance by just changing the tortilla chips on the outside. In a blue mood? Go for blue corn chips. Feeling spicy? Try Jalapeño Lime tortilla chips.

Serves
2

Temperature
380°F

Cooking Time
12 minutes

⅓ cup flour

1 teaspoon salt

1½ teaspoons chili powder

1 teaspoon ground cumin

freshly ground black pepper

1 egg, beaten

¾ cup coarsely crushed
yellow corn tortilla chips

2 (3- to 4-ounce) boneless
chicken breasts

vegetable oil

½ cup salsa

½ cup crumbled queso fresco

fresh cilantro leaves

sour cream or guacamole (optional)

1. Set up a dredging station with three shallow dishes. Combine the flour, salt, chili powder, cumin and black pepper in the first shallow dish. Beat the egg in the second shallow dish. Place the crushed tortilla chips in the third shallow dish.

2. Dredge the chicken in the spiced flour, covering all sides of the breast. Then dip the chicken into the egg, coating the chicken completely. Finally, place the chicken into the tortilla chips and press the chips onto the chicken to make sure they adhere to all sides of the breast. Spray the coated chicken breasts on both sides with vegetable oil.

3. Pre-heat the air fryer to 380°F.

4. Air-fry the chicken for 6 minutes. Then turn the chicken breasts over and air-fry for another 6 minutes. (Increase the cooking time if you are using chicken breasts larger than 3 to 4 ounces.)

5. When the chicken has finished cooking, serve each breast with a little salsa, the crumbled queso fresco and cilantro as the finishing touch. Serve some sour cream and/or guacamole at the table, if desired.

Queso fresco (literally "fresh cheese") is a cheese of Mexican origin that is bright, fresh and mild in flavor. If you can't find queso fresco in your grocery store, use a mild feta cheese or goat cheese in its place.

Thai Chicken Drumsticks

Another great feature of air-frying is that you can cook marinated foods out of their marinade, and still cook and heat the marinade to make a sauce at the same time. Here you simmer the leftover marinade from the bottom of the air fryer for just two minutes while the chicken rests and end up with a delicious sauce to pour over the finished dish.

Serves
4

Temperature
370°F

Cooking Time
20 minutes

2 tablespoons soy sauce

¼ cup rice wine vinegar

2 tablespoons chili garlic sauce

2 tablespoons sesame oil

1 teaspoon minced fresh ginger

2 teaspoons sugar

½ teaspoon ground coriander

juice of 1 lime

8 chicken drumsticks (about 2½ pounds)

¼ cup chopped peanuts

chopped fresh cilantro

lime wedges

1. Combine the soy sauce, rice wine vinegar, chili sauce, sesame oil, ginger, sugar, coriander and lime juice in a large bowl and mix together. Add the chicken drumsticks and marinate for 30 minutes.

2. Pre-heat the air fryer to 370°F.

3. Place the chicken in the air fryer basket. It's ok if the ends of the drumsticks overlap a little. Spoon half of the marinade over the chicken, and reserve the other half.

4. Air-fry for 10 minutes. Turn the chicken over and pour the rest of the marinade over the chicken. Air-fry for an additional 10 minutes.

5. Transfer the chicken to a plate to rest and cool to an edible temperature. Pour the marinade from the bottom of the air fryer into a small saucepan and bring it to a simmer over medium-high heat. Simmer the liquid for 2 minutes so that it thickens enough to coat the back of a spoon.

6. Transfer the chicken to a serving platter, pour the sauce over the chicken and sprinkle the chopped peanuts on top. Garnish with chopped cilantro and lime wedges.

If you prefer white meat to dark meat, this works well with chicken breasts too. Use bone-in chicken breasts and cook for 25 minutes, starting with the skin side down and turning the breasts over after 10 minutes. They should register 165°F on an instant read thermometer when cooked.

See photo on page 122.

Apricot Glazed Chicken Thighs

Here is a super easy recipe that is very tender and tasty. It's also really customizable – just use a different fruit preserve for a whole different dish.

Serves
2 to 4

Temperature
380°F

Cooking Time
22 minutes

4 bone-in chicken thighs (about 2 pounds)

olive oil

1 teaspoon salt

¼ teaspoon freshly ground black pepper

½ teaspoon onion powder

¾ cup apricot preserves

1½ tablespoons Dijon mustard

½ teaspoon dried thyme

1 teaspoon soy sauce

fresh thyme leaves, for garnish

1. Pre-heat the air fryer to 380°F.

2. Brush or spray both the air fryer basket and the chicken with the olive oil. Combine the salt, pepper and onion powder and season both sides of the chicken with the spice mixture.

3. Place the seasoned chicken thighs, skin side down in the air fryer basket. Air-fry for 10 minutes.

4. While chicken is cooking, make the glaze by combining the apricot preserves, Dijon mustard, thyme and soy sauce in a small bowl.

5. When the time is up on the air fryer, spoon half of the apricot glaze over the chicken thighs and air-fry for 2 minutes. Then flip the chicken thighs over so that the skin side is facing up and air-fry for an additional 8 minutes. Finally, spoon and spread the rest of the glaze evenly over the chicken thighs and air-fry for a final 2 minutes. Transfer the chicken to a serving platter and sprinkle the fresh thyme leaves on top.

Did You Know...?

The only trick to this recipe is to not let the sweet glaze burn in the air fryer. That's why the glaze is only exposed to the most intense heat for 2 minutes. So, substitute any fruit preserve that you like. Cherry preserves are especially nice on chicken.

Chicken Wellington

I'm not going to lie – this recipe has several steps, but if you want to impress someone this will do the trick! It's a restaurant quality dinner for two, but you can increase it to 4 or 6 people if you're willing to cook the Wellingtons in batches. Just hold the finished Wellingtons warm in a 170°F oven while the second batch cooks.

Serves
2

Temperature
360°F/350°F

Cooking Time
10 + 21 minutes

2 (5-ounce) boneless, skinless chicken breasts

½ cup White Worcestershire sauce

3 tablespoons butter

½ cup finely diced onion (about ½ onion)

8 ounces button mushrooms, finely chopped

¼ cup chicken stock

2 tablespoons White Worcestershire sauce (or white wine)

salt and freshly ground black pepper

1 tablespoon chopped fresh tarragon

2 sheets puff pastry, thawed

1 egg, beaten

vegetable oil

This recipe calls for White Worcestershire sauce, which you can find in the grocery store right next to the regular Worcestershire sauce. If you can't find it, don't fret – just use your favorite chicken marinade to marinate the chicken and use white wine or dry vermouth for the mushrooms.

1. Place the chicken breasts in a shallow dish. Pour the White Worcestershire sauce over the chicken coating both sides and marinate for 30 minutes.

2. While the chicken is marinating, melt the butter in a large skillet over medium-high heat on the stovetop. Add the onion and sauté for a few minutes, until it starts to soften. Add the mushrooms and sauté for 3 to 5 minutes until the vegetables are brown and soft. Deglaze the skillet with the chicken stock, scraping up any bits from the bottom of the pan. Add the White Worcestershire sauce and simmer for 2 to 3 minutes until the mixture reduces and starts to thicken. Season with salt and freshly ground black pepper. Remove the mushroom mixture from the heat and stir in the fresh tarragon. Let the mushroom mixture cool.

3. Pre-heat the air fryer to 360°F.

4. Remove the chicken from the marinade and transfer it to the air fryer basket. Tuck the small end of the chicken breast under the thicker part to shape it into a circle rather than an oval. Pour the marinade over the chicken and air-fry for 10 minutes.

5. Roll out the puff pastry and cut out two 6-inch squares. Brush the perimeter of each square with the egg wash. Place half of the mushroom mixture in the center of each puff pastry square. Place the chicken breasts, top side down on the mushroom mixture. Starting with one corner of puff pastry and working in one direction, pull the pastry up over the chicken to enclose it and press the ends of the pastry together in the middle. Brush the pastry with the egg wash to seal the edges. Turn the Wellingtons over and set aside.

6. To make a decorative design with the remaining puff pastry, cut out four 10-inch strips. For each Wellington, twist two of the strips together, place them over the chicken breast wrapped in puff pastry, and tuck the ends underneath to seal it. Brush the entire top and sides of the Wellingtons with the egg wash.

7. Pre-heat the air fryer to 350°F.

8. Spray or brush the air fryer basket with vegetable oil. Air-fry the chicken Wellingtons for 13 minutes. Carefully turn the Wellingtons over. Air-fry for another 8 minutes. Transfer to serving plates, light a candle and enjoy!

Parmesan Chicken Fingers

Here's a quick weeknight dinner that kids of all ages will love!

Serves
2 to 4

Temperature
360°F

Cooking Time
19 minutes
(9 minutes per batch + 1 minute)

½ cup flour

1 teaspoon salt

freshly ground black pepper

2 eggs, beaten

¾ cup seasoned panko breadcrumbs

¾ cup grated Parmesan cheese

8 chicken tenders (about 1 pound)

OR

2 to 3 boneless, skinless chicken breasts, cut into strips

vegetable oil

marinara sauce

1. Set up a dredging station. Combine the flour, salt and pepper in a shallow dish. Place the beaten eggs in second shallow dish, and combine the panko breadcrumbs and Parmesan cheese in a third shallow dish.

2. Dredge the chicken tenders in the flour mixture. Then dip them into the egg, and finally place the chicken in the breadcrumb mixture. Press the coating onto both sides of the chicken tenders. Place the coated chicken tenders on a baking sheet until they are all coated. Spray both sides of the chicken fingers with vegetable oil.

3. Pre-heat the air fryer to 360°F.

4. Air-fry the chicken fingers in two batches. Transfer half the chicken fingers to the air fryer basket and air-fry for 9 minutes, turning the chicken over halfway through the cooking time. When the second batch of chicken fingers has finished cooking, return the first batch to the air fryer with the second batch and air-fry for one minute to heat everything through.

5. Serve immediately with marinara sauce, honey-mustard, ketchup or your favorite dipping sauce.

Smart Tip

Parmesan chicken fingers out at a restaurant could cost you 508 calories for a serving this size. Here, you save 200 calories, with a serving calorie count of 300.

300 Calories – 11g Fat – (3g Sat. Fat)
9g Carbohydrates – 0g Fiber – 0g Sugar
39g Protein

Dress It Up

Turn this into a quick-and-easy Chicken Parmesan by shingling the cooked chicken fingers in a 7-inch cake pan, top with marinara sauce and mozzarella cheese and air-fry for 2 minutes to melt the cheese. You can also put the chicken into a toasted long roll for a fried chicken sandwich!

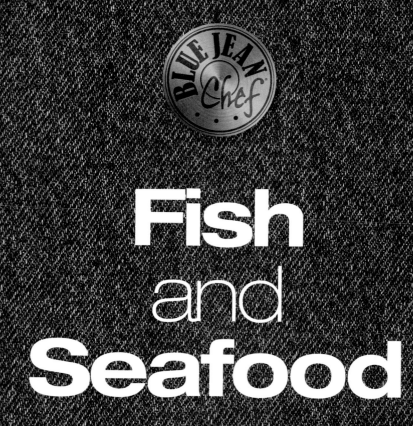

Fish and Seafood

Sea Bass
with Potato Scales and Caper Aïoli

This was a recipe created by the famous chef, Paul Bocuse, and has been done many times since. The exposed edges of the potatoes crisp up in the air fryer, but much of the potato "scale" remains tender under the layer above. It's an ingenious way of putting fish and potatoes together and it looks fantastic!

Serves
2

Temperature
400°F

Cooking Time
10 minutes

2 (6- to 8-ounce) fillets of sea bass

salt and freshly ground black pepper

¼ cup mayonnaise

2 teaspoons finely chopped lemon zest

1 teaspoon chopped fresh thyme

2 fingerling potatoes,
very thinly sliced into rounds

olive oil

½ clove garlic, crushed into a paste

1 tablespoon capers, drained and rinsed

1 tablespoon olive oil

1 teaspoon lemon juice, to taste

1. Pre-heat the air fryer to 400°F.

2. Season the fish well with salt and freshly ground black pepper. Mix the mayonnaise, lemon zest and thyme together in a small bowl. Spread a thin layer of the mayonnaise mixture on both fillets. Start layering rows of potato slices onto the fish fillets to simulate the fish scales. The second row should overlap the first row slightly. Dabbing a little more mayonnaise along the upper edge of the row of potatoes where the next row overlaps will help the potato slices stick. Press the potatoes onto the fish to secure them well and season again with salt. Brush or spray the potato layer with olive oil.

3. Transfer the fish to the air fryer and air-fry for 8 to 10 minutes, depending on the thickness of your fillets. 1-inch of fish should take 10 minutes at 400°F.

4. While the fish is cooking, add the garlic, capers, olive oil and lemon juice to the remaining mayonnaise mixture to make the caper aïoli.

5. Serve the fish warm with a dollop of the aïoli on top or on the side.

Substitution

This recipe can be done with any species of fish. You can also use red skinned or even purple potatoes for a different look, as long as the potatoes are small enough to make nice small round slices.

Black Cod
with Grapes, Fennel, Pecans and Kale

Black cod is also known as sablefish or butterfish. It's not actually part of the cod family and not similar to cod in flavor or texture. It's rich and silky and has more healthy omega-3 fatty acids than any other white fish. It's one of my favorites!

Serves
2

Temperature
400°F

Cooking Time
15 minutes

2 (6- to 8-ounce) fillets of black cod (or sablefish)

salt and freshly ground black pepper

olive oil

1 cup grapes, halved

1 small bulb fennel, sliced ¼-inch thick

½ cup pecans

3 cups shredded kale

2 teaspoons white balsamic vinegar or white wine vinegar

2 tablespoons extra virgin olive oil

1. Pre-heat the air fryer to 400°F.

2. Season the cod fillets with salt and pepper and drizzle, brush or spray a little olive oil on top. Place the fish, presentation side up (skin side down), into the air fryer basket. Air-fry for 10 minutes.

3. When the fish has finished cooking, remove the fillets to a side plate and loosely tent with foil to rest.

4. Toss the grapes, fennel and pecans in a bowl with a drizzle of olive oil and season with salt and pepper. Add the grapes, fennel and pecans to the air fryer basket and air-fry for 5 minutes at 400°F, shaking the basket once during the cooking time.

5. Transfer the grapes, fennel and pecans to a bowl with the kale. Dress the kale with the balsamic vinegar and olive oil, season to taste with salt and pepper and serve along side the cooked fish.

Did You Know...?

Fennel is a member of the carrot family. It's crunchy and sweet and has a slight licorice flavor. You can even use the pretty leaves of the fennel bulb, tossing them into the kale salad at the end. If you can't find fennel, you can use thinly sliced carrots or even crunchy celery.

Fish Sticks
with Tartar Sauce

Making these from scratch, instead of buying frozen fish sticks at the grocery store, allows you to choose what fish you'd like to use and to control all the ingredients, making it a much more healthy option, eliminating all preservatives and artificial ingredients.

Serves
2 to 3

Temperature
400°F

Cooking Time
6 minutes

12 ounces cod or flounder

½ cup flour

½ teaspoon paprika

1 teaspoon salt

lots of freshly ground black pepper

2 eggs, lightly beaten

1½ cups panko breadcrumbs

1 teaspoon salt

vegetable oil

Tartar Sauce:

¼ cup mayonnaise

2 teaspoons lemon juice

2 tablespoons finely chopped sweet pickles

salt and freshly ground black pepper

1. Cut the fish into ¾-inch wide sticks or strips. Set up a dredging station. Combine the flour, paprika, salt and pepper in a shallow dish. Beat the eggs lightly in a second shallow dish. Finally, mix the breadcrumbs and salt in a third shallow dish. Coat the fish sticks by dipping the fish into the flour, then the egg and finally the breadcrumbs, coating on all sides in each step and pressing the crumbs firmly onto the fish. Place the finished sticks on a plate or baking sheet while you finish all the sticks.

2. Pre-heat the air fryer to 400°F.

3. Spray the fish sticks with the oil and spray or brush the bottom of the air fryer basket. Place the fish into the basket and air-fry at 400°F for 4 minutes, turn the fish sticks over, and air-fry for another 2 minutes.

4. While the fish is cooking, mix the tartar sauce ingredients together.

5. Serve the fish sticks warm with the tartar sauce and some French fries on the side.

Did You Know...?

You can coat all the fish sticks and then freeze the coated fish sticks for cooking at a later date. When you do decide to cook them, just add 2 minutes onto the cooking time.

Smart Tip

Frozen fish sticks bought at the grocery store have been previously deep-fried and can have a calorie count as high as 536 calories for just the fish sticks. The same portion of air-fried fish sticks, *with* the tartar sauce comes in at 420 calories.

420 Calories – 23g Fat – (4g Sat. Fat) – 31g Carbohydrates
1g Fiber – 4g Sugar – 20g Protein

Spicy Fish Street Tacos
with Sriracha Slaw

This sriracha slaw is saucy and packs a lot of flavor, so you should not need any additional toppings on these tacos. Serve the tacos wrapped in parchment paper and everyone will think you have a gourmet taco food truck in your back yard! Great for entertaining!

Serves
2 to 3

Temperature
400°F

Cooking Time
5 minutes

Sriracha Slaw:

½ cup mayonnaise

2 tablespoons rice vinegar

1 teaspoon sugar

2 tablespoons sriracha chili sauce

5 cups shredded green cabbage

¼ cup shredded carrots

2 scallions, chopped

salt and freshly ground black pepper

Tacos:

½ cup flour

1 teaspoon chili powder

½ teaspoon ground cumin

1 teaspoon salt

freshly ground black pepper

½ teaspoon baking powder

1 egg, beaten

¼ cup milk

1 cup breadcrumbs

1 pound mahi-mahi or snapper fillets

1 tablespoon canola or vegetable oil

6 (6-inch) flour tortillas

1 lime, cut into wedges

1. Start by making the sriracha slaw. Combine the mayonnaise, rice vinegar, sugar, and sriracha sauce in a large bowl. Mix well and add the green cabbage, carrots, and scallions. Toss until all the vegetables are coated with the dressing and season with salt and pepper. Refrigerate the slaw until you are ready to serve the tacos.

2. Combine the flour, chili powder, cumin, salt, pepper and baking powder in a bowl. Add the egg and milk and mix until the batter is smooth. Place the breadcrumbs in shallow dish.

3. Cut the fish fillets into 1-inch wide sticks, approximately 4-inches long. You should have about 12 fish sticks total. Dip the fish sticks into the batter, coating all sides. Let the excess batter drip off the fish and then roll them in the breadcrumbs, patting the crumbs onto all sides of the fish sticks. Set the coated fish on a plate or baking sheet until all the fish has been coated.

4. Pre-heat the air fryer to 400°F.

5. Spray the coated fish sticks with oil on all sides. Spray or brush the inside of the air fryer basket with oil and transfer the fish to the basket. Place as many sticks as you can in one layer, leaving a little room around each stick. Place any remaining sticks on top, perpendicular to the first layer.

6. Air-fry the fish for 3 minutes. Turn the fish sticks over and air-fry for an additional 2 minutes.

7. While the fish is air-frying, warm the tortilla shells either in a 350°F oven wrapped in foil or in a skillet with a little oil over medium-high heat for a couple minutes. Fold the tortillas in half and keep them warm until the remaining tortillas and fish are ready.

8. To assemble the tacos, place two pieces of the fish in each tortilla shell and top with the sriracha slaw. Squeeze the lime wedge over top and dig in.

Fish and "Chips"

The "chips" in this recipe are not the sort you dip in ketchup! They are salt and vinegar chips used as a coating for the fish, giving you the classic salty and vinegary flavor of fish and chips all in one bite.

Serves
2 to 3

Temperature
370°F

Cooking Time
10 minutes

½ cup flour

½ teaspoon paprika

¼ teaspoon ground white pepper
(or freshly ground black pepper)

1 egg

¼ cup mayonnaise

2 cups salt & vinegar kettle cooked
potato chips, coarsely crushed

12 ounces cod

tartar sauce

lemon wedges

1. Set up a dredging station. Combine the flour, paprika and pepper in a shallow dish. Combine the egg and mayonnaise in a second shallow dish. Place the crushed potato chips in a third shallow dish.

2. Cut the cod into 6 pieces. Dredge each piece of fish in the flour, then dip it into the egg mixture and then place it into the crushed potato chips. Make sure all sides of the fish are covered and pat the chips gently onto the fish so they stick well.

3. Pre-heat the air fryer to 370°F.

4. Place the coated fish fillets into the air fry basket. (It is ok if a couple of pieces slightly overlap or rest on top of other fillets in order to fit everything in the basket.)

5. Air-fry for 10 minutes, gently turning the fish over halfway through the cooking time.

6. Transfer the fish to a platter and serve with tartar sauce and lemon wedges.

Tartar Sauce

1 cup mayonnaise

⅓ cup dill pickle relish

2 tablespoons capers, rinsed and chopped

1 tablespoon lemon juice

dash cayenne pepper

salt and freshly ground black pepper

1. Mix all the ingredients together in a bowl. Season to taste with salt and freshly ground black pepper and serve.

Maple Balsamic Glazed Salmon

Fish is so delicious in the air fryer because it stays so moist! This super easy recipe finishes simply air-fried salmon with a sweet glaze at the end. Couldn't be any easier!

Serves
4

Temperature
400°F

Cooking Time
10 minutes

4 (6-ounce) fillets of salmon

salt and freshly ground black pepper

vegetable oil

¼ cup pure maple syrup

3 tablespoons balsamic vinegar

1 teaspoon Dijon mustard

1. Pre-heat the air fryer to 400ºF.

2. Season the salmon well with salt and freshly ground black pepper. Spray or brush the bottom of the air fryer basket with vegetable oil and place the salmon fillets inside. Air-fry the salmon for 5 minutes.

3. While the salmon is air-frying, combine the maple syrup, balsamic vinegar and Dijon mustard in a small saucepan over medium heat and stir to blend well. Let the mixture simmer while the fish is cooking. It should start to thicken slightly, but keep your eye on it so it doesn't burn.

4. Brush the glaze on the salmon fillets and air-fry for an additional 5 minutes. The salmon should feel firm to the touch when finished and the glaze should be nicely browned on top. Brush a little more glaze on top before removing and serving with rice and vegetables, or a nice green salad.

The quality of your finished dish is directly related to the quality of your ingredients. So, especially when a recipe calls for very few ingredients, make sure those ingredients are of the highest quality. Make sure your salmon is as fresh as possible. Use pure maple syrup instead of a blend, and use balsamic vinegar that is at least 6% acidity. As for Dijon mustard, well use the one you like the best!

Coconut Shrimp

This delicious crunchy shrimp dish will be a big hit at your next gathering! The coconut is just subtle enough to keep you guessing, the lime zest brightens it all up and the cayenne gives it some zing. All together, it just keeps you going back for more!

Serves
4

Temperature
400°F/340°F

Cooking Time
12 minutes
(5 minutes per batch + 2 minutes)

1 pound large shrimp (about 16 to 20), peeled and de-veined

½ cup flour

salt and freshly ground black pepper

2 egg whites

½ cup fine breadcrumbs

½ cup shredded unsweetened coconut

zest of one lime

½ teaspoon salt

⅛ to ¼ teaspoon ground cayenne pepper

vegetable or canola oil

sweet chili sauce or duck sauce
(for serving)

1. Set up a dredging station. Place the flour in a shallow dish and season well with salt and freshly ground black pepper. Whisk the egg whites in a second shallow dish. In a third shallow dish, combine the breadcrumbs, coconut, lime zest, salt and cayenne pepper.

2. Pre-heat the air fryer to 400°F.

3. Dredge each shrimp first in the flour, then dip it in the egg mixture, and finally press it into the breadcrumb-coconut mixture to coat all sides. Place the breaded shrimp on a plate or baking sheet and spray both sides with vegetable oil.

4. Air-fry the shrimp in two batches, being sure not to over-crowd the basket. Air-fry for 5 minutes, turning the shrimp over for the last minute or two. Repeat with the second batch of shrimp.

5. Lower the temperature of the air fryer to 340°F. Return the first batch of shrimp to the air fryer basket with the second batch and air-fry for an additional 1 to 2 minutes, just to re-heat everything.

6. Serve with sweet chili sauce, duck sauce or just eat them plain!

Did You Know...?

Shrimp are sized and categorized into groups based on how many are in a pound. When you see numbers like 16/20 on shrimp, it means there are between 16 and 20 shrimp per pound. That's convenient for home cooks, who can generally estimate how many shrimp each person will eat.

Smart Tip

Coconut shrimp from your favorite fast food restaurant can contain as many as 636 calories. This version has just 230 calories per serving.

420 Calories – 23g Fat – (4g Sat. Fat) – 31g Carbohydrates
1g Fiber – 4g Sugar – 20g Protein

Crab Cakes

It's true! You can make restaurant quality crab cakes at home in ten minutes!

Serves
2 to 4

Temperature
400°F

Cooking Time
10 minutes

1 teaspoon butter

⅓ cup finely diced onion

⅓ cup finely diced celery

¼ cup mayonnaise

1 teaspoon Dijon mustard

1 egg

pinch ground cayenne pepper

1 teaspoon salt

freshly ground black pepper

16 ounces lump crabmeat

½ cup + 2 tablespoons panko breadcrumbs, divided

1. Melt the butter in a skillet over medium heat. Sauté the onion and celery until it starts to soften, but not brown – about 4 minutes. Transfer the cooked vegetables to a large bowl. Add the mayonnaise, Dijon mustard, egg, cayenne pepper, salt and freshly ground black pepper to the bowl. Gently fold in the lump crabmeat and 2 tablespoons of panko breadcrumbs. Stir carefully so you don't break up all the crab pieces.

2. Pre-heat the air fryer to 400°F.

3. Place the remaining panko breadcrumbs in a shallow dish. Divide the crab mixture into 4 portions and shape each portion into a round patty. Dredge the crab patties in the breadcrumbs, coating both sides as well as the edges with the crumbs.

4. Air-fry the crab cakes for 5 minutes. Using a flat spatula, gently turn the cakes over and air-fry for another 5 minutes. Serve the crab cakes with tartar sauce or cocktail sauce, or dress it up with the suggestion below.

Dress It Up

You can dress these cakes up with the following simple sauce, easy to do while the crab cakes cook.

Sherry Sauce

2 tablespoons butter, divided

1 shallot, minced

½ cup dry sherry

½ cup heavy cream

1 teaspoon Dijon mustard

salt and freshly ground black pepper

½ teaspoon chopped fresh tarragon

1. Melt one tablespoon of butter in a small saucepan over medium heat. Sauté the shallot until it just starts to brown. Pour in the sherry and scrape up any brown bits on the bottom of the pan. Simmer until the liquid has reduced by half. Add the heavy cream and Dijon mustard and continue to simmer until the sauce thickens. Season to taste with salt and freshly ground black pepper.

2. If you want a very smooth sauce, strain the sauce through a fine strainer before proceeding. Otherwise, just stir in the remaining butter and tarragon and serve.

Nutty Shrimp with Amaretto Glaze

The glaze on this shrimp appetizer has just one ingredient so it truly couldn't be easier to make! This recipe assumes you are making hors d'oeuvres for a crowd. You can easily cut the quantities in half to feed fewer people and not air-fry as many batches.

Serves
10 to 12 (as an appetizer)

Temperature
400°F

Cooking Time
40 to 50 minutes
(10 minutes per batch)

1 cup flour

½ teaspoon baking powder

1 teaspoon salt

2 eggs, beaten

½ cup milk

2 tablespoons olive or vegetable oil

2 cups sliced almonds

2 pounds large shrimp
(about 32 to 40 shrimp),
peeled and deveined, tails left on

2 cups amaretto liqueur

1. Combine the flour, baking powder and salt in a large bowl. Add the eggs, milk and oil and stir until it forms a smooth batter. Coarsely crush the sliced almonds into a second shallow dish with your hands.

2. Dry the shrimp well with paper towels. Dip the shrimp into the batter and shake off any excess batter, leaving just enough to lightly coat the shrimp. Transfer the shrimp to the dish with the almonds and coat completely. Place the coated shrimp on a plate or baking sheet and when all the shrimp have been coated, freeze the shrimp for an 1 hour, or as long as a week before air-frying.

3. Pre-heat the air fryer to 400°F.

4. Transfer 8 frozen shrimp at a time to the air fryer basket. Air-fry for 6 minutes. Turn the shrimp over and air-fry for an additional 4 minutes. Repeat with the remaining shrimp.

5. While the shrimp are cooking, bring the Amaretto to a boil in a small saucepan on the stovetop. Lower the heat and simmer until it has reduced and thickened into a glaze – about 10 minutes.

6. Remove the shrimp from the air fryer and brush both sides with the warm amaretto glaze. Serve warm.

Did You Know…?

You can prepare this shrimp ahead of time if you're planning a party. Cook the shrimp all the way through but don't glaze them. Then, when you're ready to serve them, re-heat the cooked shrimp at 330°F for 1 to 2 minutes and then brush with the amaretto glaze.

Lemon-Dill Salmon Burgers

This burger is quick, delicious and a nice change from the regular beef burger. I stick to my rule of thumb for the success of any meal with this burger – the best ingredients will give you the best results. So, pick up two high-quality fresh fillets of salmon for this dinner for four.

Serves
4

Temperature
400°F

Cooking Time
8 minutes

2 (6-ounce) fillets of salmon, finely chopped by hand or in a food processor

1 cup fine breadcrumbs

1 teaspoon freshly grated lemon zest

2 tablespoons chopped fresh dill weed

1 teaspoon salt

freshly ground black pepper

2 eggs, lightly beaten

4 brioche or hamburger buns

lettuce, tomato, red onion, avocado, mayonnaise or mustard, to serve

1. Pre-heat the air fryer to 400°F.

2. Combine all the ingredients in a bowl. Mix together well and divide into four balls. Flatten the balls into patties, making an indentation in the center of each patty with your thumb (this will help the burger stay flat as it cooks) and flattening the sides of the burgers so that they fit nicely into the air fryer basket.

3. Transfer the burgers to the air fryer basket and air-fry for 4 minutes. Flip the burgers over and air-fry for another 3 to 4 minutes, until nicely browned and firm to the touch.

4. Serve on soft brioche buns with your choice of topping – lettuce, tomato, red onion, avocado, mayonnaise or mustard.

Dress It Up

If you want to enhance the lemon-dill flavor of this burger, serve it with lemon-dill mayonnaise.

Lemon-Dill Mayonnaise

¼ cup mayonnaise

1 teaspoon lemon juice

1 teaspoon lemon zest

2 tablespoons finely chopped dill weed

salt and freshly ground black pepper

1. Mix all the ingredients together in a bowl and spread the mixture on the buns before serving.

Vegetarian Main Dishes

Cauliflower Steaks Gratin

This can be served as the center of the plate of a vegetarian meal, or a generous side dish for a non-vegetarian meal. Look for a tight head of cauliflower so that the steak you make has a lot of surface area.

Serves
2

Temperature
370°F

Cooking Time
13 minutes

1 head cauliflower

1 tablespoon olive oil

salt and freshly ground black pepper

½ teaspoon chopped fresh thyme leaves

3 tablespoons grated Parmigiano-Reggiano cheese

2 tablespoons panko breadcrumbs

1. Pre-heat the air-fryer to 370°F.

2. Cut two steaks out of the center of the cauliflower. To do this, cut the cauliflower in half and then cut one slice about 1-inch thick off each half. The rest of the cauliflower will fall apart into florets, which you can roast on their own or save for another meal.

3. Brush both sides of the cauliflower steaks with olive oil and season with salt, freshly ground black pepper and fresh thyme. Place the cauliflower steaks into the air fryer basket and air-fry for 6 minutes. Turn the steaks over and air-fry for another 4 minutes. Combine the Parmesan cheese and panko breadcrumbs and sprinkle the mixture over the tops of both steaks and air-fry for another 3 minutes until the cheese has melted and the breadcrumbs have browned. Serve this with some sautéed bitter greens and air-fried blistered tomatoes.

Dress It Up

You will have some leftover florets with this recipe and a nice way to incorporate them into this meal is to blanch them and purée them with a little milk or half and half, salt and pepper. Serve the tender cauliflower steak with its crunchy surface, on top of the smooth purée.

Roasted Vegetable Lasagna

This recipe is a nice light change from traditional lasagna. It's full of roasted vegetables that you can choose to suit your own tastes and instead of a marinara, the sauce in this lasagna is a creamy white béchamel sauce.

Serves
6

Temperature
400°F

Cooking Time
10 + 45 minutes

1 zucchini, sliced

1 yellow squash, sliced

8 ounces mushrooms, sliced

1 red bell pepper, cut into 2-inch strips

1 tablespoon olive oil

2 cups ricotta cheese

2 cups grated mozzarella cheese, divided

1 egg

1 teaspoon salt

freshly ground black pepper

¼ cup shredded carrots

½ cup chopped fresh spinach

8 lasagna noodles, cooked

Béchamel Sauce:

3 tablespoons butter

3 tablespoons flour

2½ cups milk

½ cup grated Parmesan cheese

½ teaspoon salt

freshly ground black pepper

pinch of ground nutmeg

See photo on page 162.

1. Pre-heat the air fryer to 400°F.

2. Toss the zucchini, yellow squash, mushrooms and red pepper in a large bowl with the olive oil and season with salt and pepper. Air-fry for 10 minutes, shaking the basket once or twice while the vegetables cook.

3. While the vegetables are cooking, make the béchamel sauce and cheese filling. Melt the butter in a medium saucepan over medium-high heat on the stovetop. Add the flour and whisk, cooking for a couple of minutes. Add the milk and whisk vigorously until smooth. Bring the mixture to a boil and simmer until the sauce thickens. Stir in the Parmesan cheese and season with the salt, pepper and nutmeg. Set the sauce aside.

4. Combine the ricotta cheese, 1¼ cups of the mozzarella cheese, egg, salt and pepper in a large bowl and stir until combined. Fold in the carrots and spinach.

5. When the vegetables have finished cooking, build the lasagna. Use a baking dish that is 6 inches in diameter and 4 inches high. Cover the bottom of the baking dish with a little béchamel sauce. Top with two lasagna noodles, cut to fit the dish and overlapping each other a little. Spoon a third of the ricotta cheese mixture and then a third of the roasted veggies on top of the noodles. Pour ½ cup of béchamel sauce on top and then repeat these layers two more times: noodles – cheese mixture – vegetables – béchamel sauce. Sprinkle the remaining mozzarella cheese over the top. Cover the dish with aluminum foil, tenting it loosely so the aluminum doesn't touch the cheese.

6. Lower the dish into the air fryer basket using an aluminum foil sling (fold a piece of aluminum foil into a strip about 2-inches wide by 24-inches long). Fold the ends of the aluminum foil over the top of the dish before returning the basket to the air fryer. Air-fry for 45 minutes, removing the foil for the last 2 minutes, to slightly brown the cheese on top.

7. Let the lasagna rest for at least 20 minutes to set up a little before slicing into it and serving.

Falafel

You can wrap these little fried chickpea balls in a pita bread for a sandwich, or serve them on top of a salad or even as part of an appetizer tray. These are best made from dried chickpeas that are soaked overnight, so this recipe does require a little planning. If planning is not your forte, you can use 2 (15-ounce) cans of chickpeas, but do make sure you dry them as well as you can.

Serves
4

Temperature
380°F

Cooking Time
10 minutes

1 cup dried chickpeas

½ onion, chopped

1 clove garlic

¼ cup fresh parsley leaves

1 teaspoon salt

¼ teaspoon crushed red pepper flakes

1 teaspoon ground cumin

½ teaspoon ground coriander

1 to 2 tablespoons flour

olive oil

Tomato Salad

2 tomatoes, seeds removed and diced

½ cucumber, finely diced

¼ red onion, finely diced and rinsed with water

1 teaspoon red wine vinegar

1 tablespoon olive oil

salt and freshly ground black pepper

2 tablespoons chopped fresh parsley

1. Cover the chickpeas with water and let them soak overnight on the counter. Then drain the chickpeas and put them in a food processor, along with the onion, garlic, parsley, spices and 1 tablespoon of flour. Pulse in the food processor until the mixture has broken down into a coarse paste consistency. The mixture should hold together when you pinch it. Add more flour as needed, until you get this consistency.

2. Scoop portions of the mixture (about 2 tablespoons in size) and shape into balls. Place the balls on a plate and refrigerate for at least 30 minutes. You should have between 12 and 14 balls.

3. Pre-heat the air fryer to 380ºF.

4. Spray the falafel balls with oil and place them in the air fryer. Air-fry for 10 minutes, rolling them over and spraying them with oil again halfway through the cooking time so that they cook and brown evenly.

5. Serve with pita bread, hummus, cucumbers, hot peppers, tomatoes or any other fillings you might like.

Dress It Up

Dress up your falafel sandwich with the cucumber yogurt dip on page 120 along with this easy tomato salad. Just mix all ingredients together and toss.

Spinach and Cheese Calzone

A calzone is a stuffed folded pizza filled with cheeses and any other ingredient that suits your fancy. They can be baked or fried, so why not prepare them with the best of both worlds – in the air fryer!

Serves
2

Temperature
360°F

Cooking Time
20 minutes
(10 minutes per calzone)

⅔ cup frozen chopped spinach, thawed

1 cup grated mozzarella cheese

1 cup ricotta cheese

½ teaspoon Italian seasoning

½ teaspoon salt

freshly ground black pepper

1 store-bought or homemade pizza dough*
(about 12 to 16 ounces)

2 tablespoons olive oil

pizza or marinara sauce (optional)

* One batch of the Blue Jean Chef pizza dough on page 231 will make three calzones.

1. Drain and squeeze all the water out of the thawed spinach and set it aside. Mix the mozzarella cheese, ricotta cheese, Italian seasoning, salt and freshly ground black pepper together in a bowl. Stir in the chopped spinach.

2. Divide the dough in half. With floured hands or on a floured surface, stretch or roll one half of the dough into a 10-inch circle. Spread half of the cheese and spinach mixture on half of the dough, leaving about one inch of dough empty around the edge.

3. Fold the other half of the dough over the cheese mixture, almost to the edge of the bottom dough to form a half moon. Fold the bottom edge of dough up over the top edge and crimp the dough around the edges in order to make the crust and seal the calzone. Brush the dough with olive oil. Repeat with the second half of dough to make the second calzone.

4. Pre-heat the air fryer to 360°F.

5. Brush or spray the air fryer basket with olive oil. Air-fry the calzones one at a time for 10 minutes, flipping the calzone over half way through. Serve with warm pizza or marinara sauce if desired.

Substitution

Make this calzone your own! Substitute 1 cup of any filling of your choice in place of the spinach in this recipe. Try blanched broccoli, sautéed mushrooms, sun-dried tomatoes or a combination of ingredients.

Roasted Vegetable Stromboli

This delicious dinner for two (or snack for many) is so versatile. You can swap out the fillings to include anything you like as long as the ingredients are cooked ahead of time.

Serves
2

Temperature
400°F/360°F

Cooking Time
14 + 15 minutes

½ onion, thinly sliced

½ red pepper, julienned

½ yellow pepper, julienned

olive oil

1 small zucchini, thinly sliced

1 cup thinly sliced mushrooms

1½ cups chopped broccoli

1 teaspoon Italian seasoning

salt and freshly ground black pepper

½ recipe of Blue Jean Chef Pizza dough (page 231)
OR
1 (14-ounce) tube refrigerated pizza dough

2 cups grated mozzarella cheese

¼ cup grated Parmesan cheese

½ cup sliced black olives, optional

dried oregano

pizza or marinara sauce

1. Pre-heat the air fryer to 400°F.

2. Toss the onions and peppers with a little olive oil and air-fry the vegetables for 7 minutes, shaking the basket once or twice while the vegetables cook. Add the zucchini, mushrooms, broccoli and Italian seasoning to the basket. Add a little more olive oil and season with salt and freshly ground black pepper. Air-fry for an additional 7 minutes, shaking the basket halfway through. Let the vegetables cool slightly while you roll out the pizza dough.

3. On a lightly floured surface, roll or press the pizza dough out into a 13-inch by 11-inch rectangle, with the long side closest to you. Sprinkle half of the mozzarella and Parmesan cheeses over the dough leaving an empty 1-inch border from the edge farthest away from you. Spoon the roasted vegetables over the cheese, sprinkle the olives (if using) over everything and top with the remaining cheese.

4. Start rolling the stromboli away from you and toward the empty border. Make sure the filling stays tightly tucked inside the roll. Finally, tuck the ends of the dough in and pinch the seam shut. Place the seam side down and shape the stromboli into a U-shape to fit into the air fryer basket. Cut 4 small slits with the tip of a sharp knife evenly in the top of the dough, lightly brush the stromboli with a little oil and sprinkle with some dried oregano.

5. Pre-heat the air fryer to 360°F.

6. Spray or brush the air fryer basket with oil and transfer the U-shaped stromboli to the air fryer basket. Air-fry for 15 minutes, flipping the stromboli over after the first 10 minutes. (Use a plate to invert the Stromboli out of the air fryer basket and then slide it back into the basket off the plate.)

7. To remove, carefully flip the stromboli over onto a cutting board. Let it rest for a couple of minutes before serving. Cut it into 2-inch slices and serve with pizza or marinara sauce.

Stuffed Zucchini Boats

This is a great recipe for the summer when zucchini are abundant in the farmers' markets or perhaps in your own garden. Stuffed vegetable dishes usually call for cooked rice or quinoa or other cooked grain. If you don't happen to have any leftovers on hand, that can really extend your cooking time. Couscous, on the other hand, cooks in about 5 minutes – a quick and easy ingredient for these stuffed zucchini boats.

Serves
2

Temperature
380°F

Cooking Time
20 minutes

olive oil

½ cup onion, finely chopped

1 clove garlic, finely minced

½ teaspoon dried oregano

¼ teaspoon dried thyme

¾ cup couscous

1½ cups chicken stock, divided

1 tomato, seeds removed
and finely chopped

½ cup coarsely chopped Kalamata olives

½ cup grated Romano cheese

¼ cup pine nuts, toasted

1 tablespoon chopped fresh parsley

1 teaspoon salt

freshly ground black pepper

1 egg, beaten

1 cup grated mozzarella cheese, divided

2 thick zucchini

1. Pre-heat a sauté pan on the stovetop over medium-high heat. Add the olive oil and sauté the onion until it just starts to soften– about 4 minutes. Stir in the garlic, dried oregano and thyme. Add the couscous and sauté for just a minute. Add 1¼ cups of the chicken stock and simmer over low heat for 3 to 5 minutes, until liquid has been absorbed and the couscous is soft. Remove the pan from heat and set it aside to cool slightly.

2. Fluff the couscous and add the tomato, Kalamata olives, Romano cheese, pine nuts, parsley, salt and pepper. Mix well. Add the remaining chicken stock, the egg and ½ cup of the mozzarella cheese. Stir to ensure everything is combined.

3. Cut each zucchini in half lengthwise. Then, trim each half of the zucchini into four 5-inch lengths. (Save the trimmed ends of the zucchini for another use.) Use a spoon to scoop out the center of the zucchini, leaving some flesh around the sides. Brush both sides of the zucchini with olive oil and season the cut side with salt and pepper.

4. Pre-heat the air fryer to 380ºF.

5. Divide the couscous filling between the four zucchini boats. Use your hands to press the filling together and fill the inside of the zucchini. The filling should be mounded into the boats and rounded on top.

6. Transfer the zucchini boats to the air fryer basket and drizzle the stuffed zucchini boats with olive oil. Air-fry for 19 minutes. Then, sprinkle the remaining mozzarella cheese on top of the zucchini, pressing it down onto the filling lightly to prevent it from blowing around in the air fryer. Air-fry for one more minute to melt the cheese. Transfer the finished zucchini boats to a serving platter and garnish with the chopped parsley.

Substitution

Of course, if you do happen to have leftover rice or quinoa, you can use either in place of the couscous in this recipe. You will need roughly 2½ to 3 cups cooked rice or quinoa.

Eggplant Parmesan

This is another dish that takes a little while to assemble, but cooking this in the air fryer has several advantages. First of all, you are air-frying the eggplant with very little oil, which is a healthier option, and creates no splatter on the stovetop. Secondly, you can bake the assembled casserole without turning on your big oven, helping to keep your kitchen cool.

Serves
4 to 6

Temperature
400°F/350°F

Cooking Time
15 minutes per batch of eggplant
+ 35 minutes

1 medium eggplant (about 1 pound),
cut into ½-inch slices

kosher salt

½ cup breadcrumbs

2 teaspoons dried parsley

½ teaspoon Italian seasoning

½ teaspoon garlic powder

½ teaspoon onion powder

½ teaspoon salt

freshly ground black pepper

2 tablespoons milk

½ cup mayonnaise

1 cup tomato sauce

1 (14-ounce) can diced tomatoes

1 teaspoon Italian seasoning

2 cups grated mozzarella cheese

½ cup grated Parmesan cheese

1. Lay the eggplant slices on a baking sheet and sprinkle kosher salt generously over the top. Let the eggplant sit for 15 minutes while you prepare the rest of the ingredients.

2. Prepare a dredging station. Combine the breadcrumbs, parsley, Italian seasoning, garlic powder, onion powder, salt and black pepper in a shallow dish. Whisk the milk and mayonnaise together in a small bowl until smooth.

3. Pre-heat the air fryer to 400ºF.

4. Brush the excess salt from the eggplant slices and then coat both sides of each slice with the mayonnaise mixture. Dip the eggplant into the breadcrumbs, pressing the crumbs on to coat both sides of each slice. Place all the coated eggplant slices on a plate or baking sheet and spray both sides with olive oil. Air-fry the eggplant slices in batches for 15 minutes, turning them over halfway through the cooking time.

5. While the eggplant is cooking, prepare the components of the eggplant Parmesan. Mix the tomato sauce, diced tomatoes and Italian seasoning in a bowl. Combine the mozzarella and Parmesan cheeses in a second bowl.

6. Once all of the eggplant has been browned, build the dish with all the ingredient components. Cover the bottom of a 1½-quart round baking dish (6-inches in diameter) with a few tablespoons of the tomato sauce mixture. Top with one third of the eggplant slices, one third of the tomato sauce and then one third of the cheese. Repeat these layers two more times, finishing with cheese on top. Cover the dish with aluminum foil and transfer the dish to the basket of the air fryer, lowering the dish into the basket using a sling made of aluminum foil (fold a piece of aluminum foil into a strip about 2-inches wide by 24-inches long). Fold the ends of the aluminum foil over the top of the dish before returning the basket to the air fryer.

7. Air-fry at 350ºF for 30 minutes. Remove the foil and air-fry for an additional 5 minutes to brown the cheese on top. Let the eggplant Parmesan rest for a few minutes to set up and cool to an edible temperature before serving.

Broccoli Cheddar Stuffed Potatoes

When I lived in San Francisco there was a small quick-service restaurant in my neighborhood that served nothing but stuffed potatoes. It was a fun place to go and dinner was always satisfying. A stuffed potato can be varied so easily with so many different fillings. You can also vary the size of dinner by choosing the right sized potato for the occasion.

Serves
2

Temperature
400°F/360°F/330°F

Cooking Time
42 minutes

2 large russet potatoes, scrubbed

1 tablespoon olive oil

salt and freshly ground black pepper

2 tablespoons butter

¼ cup sour cream

3 tablespoons half-and-half (or milk)

1¼ cups grated Cheddar cheese, divided

¾ teaspoon salt

freshly ground black pepper

1 cup frozen baby broccoli florets, thawed and drained

1. Pre-heat the air fryer to 400°F.

2. Rub the potatoes all over with olive oil and season generously with salt and freshly ground black pepper. Transfer the potatoes into the air fryer basket and air-fry for 30 minutes, turning the potatoes over halfway through the cooking process.

3. Remove the potatoes from the air fryer and let them rest for 5 minutes. Cut a large oval out of the top of both potatoes. Leaving half an inch of potato flesh around the edge of the potato, scoop the inside of the potato out and into a large bowl to prepare the potato filling. Mash the scooped potato filling with a fork and add the butter, sour cream, half-and-half, 1 cup of the grated Cheddar cheese, salt and pepper to taste. Mix well and then fold in the broccoli florets.

4. Stuff the hollowed out potato shells with the potato and broccoli mixture. Mound the filling high in the potatoes – you will have more filling than room in the potato shells.

5. Transfer the stuffed potatoes back to the air fryer basket and air-fry at 360°F for 10 minutes. Sprinkle the remaining Cheddar cheese on top of each stuffed potato, lower the heat to 330°F and air-fry for an additional minute or two to melt cheese.

Substitution

If you can't find frozen baby broccoli florets, you can use regular frozen broccoli chopped into smaller pieces. If you'd prefer to use fresh broccoli, blanch the broccoli florets first in salted boiling water before incorporating them into the potato filling.

Mushroom, Zucchini and Black Bean Burgers

There are so many varieties of veggie burgers out there. This is one of my favorites. I love the bright flavor of lemon and cilantro next to the earthiness of the mushrooms and black beans. You can serve these on any bun you like. I especially like them in a whole-wheat pita, but they are also delicious on brioche or alone with a side salad.

Serves
4

Temperature
400°F/370°F

Cooking Time
30 minutes
(6 minutes + 12 minutes per batch)

1 cup diced zucchini,
(about ½ medium zucchini)

1 tablespoon olive oil

salt and freshly ground black pepper

1 cup chopped brown mushrooms
(about 3 ounces)

1 small clove garlic

1 (15-ounce) can black beans,
drained and rinsed

1 teaspoon lemon zest

1 tablespoon chopped fresh cilantro

½ cup plain breadcrumbs

1 egg, beaten

½ teaspoon salt

freshly ground black pepper

whole-wheat pita bread, burger buns
or brioche buns

mayonnaise, tomato, avocado
and lettuce, for serving

1. Pre-heat the air fryer to 400°F.

2. Toss the zucchini with the olive oil, season with salt and freshly ground black pepper and air-fry for 6 minutes, shaking the basket once or twice while it cooks.

3. Transfer the zucchini to a food processor with the mushrooms, garlic and black beans and process until still a little chunky but broken down and pasty. Transfer the mixture to a bowl. Add the lemon zest, cilantro, breadcrumbs and egg and mix well. Season again with salt and freshly ground black pepper. Shape the mixture into four burger patties and refrigerate for at least 15 minutes.

4. Pre-heat the air fryer to 370°F. Transfer two of the veggie burgers to the air fryer basket and air-fry for 12 minutes, flipping the burgers gently halfway through the cooking time. Keep the burgers warm by loosely tenting them with foil while you cook the remaining two burgers. Return the first batch of burgers back into the air fryer with the second batch for the last two minutes of cooking to re-heat.

5. Serve on toasted whole-wheat pita bread, burger buns or brioche buns with some mayonnaise, tomato, avocado and lettuce.

Substitution

Try this recipe using chickpeas instead of black beans for a tasty variation.

Curried Potato, Cauliflower and Pea Turnovers

This recipe takes a little work, but if you have the time there's a reward at the end. These are very much like large samosas – the popular Indian appetizer. Serve these turnovers with a carrot salad or some curried chickpeas

Serves
4

Temperature
380°F

Cooking Time
40 minutes
(20 minutes per batch)

Dough:

2 cups all-purpose flour

½ teaspoon baking powder

1 teaspoon salt

freshly ground black pepper

¼ teaspoon dried thyme

¼ cup canola oil

½ to ⅔ cup water

Turnover Filling:

1 tablespoon canola or vegetable oil

1 onion, finely chopped

1 clove garlic, minced

1 tablespoon grated fresh ginger

½ teaspoon cumin seeds

½ teaspoon fennel seeds

1 teaspoon curry powder

2 russet potatoes, diced

2 cups cauliflower florets

½ cup frozen peas

2 tablespoons chopped fresh cilantro

salt and freshly ground black pepper

2 tablespoons butter, melted

mango chutney, for serving

1. Start by making the dough. Combine the flour, baking powder, salt, pepper and dried thyme in a mixing bowl or the bowl of a stand mixer. Drizzle in the canola oil and pinch it together with your fingers to turn the flour into a crumby mixture. Stir in the water (enough to bring the dough together). Knead the dough for 5 minutes or so until it is smooth. Add a little more water or flour as needed. Let the dough rest while you make the turnover filling.

2. Pre-heat a large skillet on the stovetop over medium-high heat. Add the oil and sauté the onion until it starts to become tender – about 4 minutes. Add the garlic and ginger and continue to cook for another minute. Add the dried spices and toss everything to coat. Add the potatoes and cauliflower to the skillet and pour in 1½ cups of water. Simmer everything together for 20 to 25 minutes, or until the potatoes are soft and most of the water has evaporated. If the water has evaporated and the vegetables still need more time, just add a little water and continue to simmer until everything is tender. Stir well, crushing the potatoes and cauliflower a little as you do so. Stir in the peas and cilantro, season to taste with salt and freshly ground black pepper and set aside to cool.

3. Divide the dough into 4 balls. Roll the dough balls out into ¼-inch thick circles. Divide the cooled potato filling between the dough circles, placing a mound of the filling on one side of each piece of dough, leaving an empty border around the edge of the dough. Brush the edges of the dough with a little water and fold one edge of circle over the filling to meet the other edge of the circle, creating a half moon. Pinch the edges together with your fingers and then press the edge with the tines of a fork to decorate and seal.

4. Pre-heat the air fryer to 380ºF.

5. Spray or brush the air fryer basket with oil. Brush the turnovers with the melted butter and place 2 turnovers into the air fryer basket. Air-fry for 15 minutes. Flip the turnovers over and air-fry for another 5 minutes. Repeat with the remaining 2 turnovers.

6. These will be very hot when they come out of the air fryer. Let them cool for at least 20 minutes before serving warm with mango chutney.

Asparagus, Mushroom and Cheese Soufflés

The ingredient responsible for this soufflé's decadent flavor and smooth texture is the Gruyère cheese. While you can use other Swiss cheeses instead of Gruyère, try not to compromise on the quality of the cheese. A Comté or Beaufort cheese would be really nice, but Gruyère is easier to find.

Serves
3

Temperature
400°F/330°F

Cooking Time
7 + 14 minutes

butter

grated Parmesan cheese

3 button mushrooms, thinly sliced

8 spears asparagus, sliced ½-inch long

1 teaspoon olive oil

1 tablespoon butter

4½ teaspoons flour

pinch paprika

pinch ground nutmeg

salt and freshly ground black pepper

½ cup milk

½ cup grated Gruyère cheese
or other Swiss cheese (about 2 ounces)

2 eggs, separated

1. Butter three 6-ounce ramekins and dust with grated Parmesan cheese. (Butter the ramekins and then coat the butter with Parmesan by shaking it around in the ramekin and dumping out any excess.)

2. Pre-heat the air fryer to 400°F.

3. Toss the mushrooms and asparagus in a bowl with the olive oil. Transfer the vegetables to the air fryer and air-fry for 7 minutes, shaking the basket once or twice to redistribute the ingredients while they cook.

4. While the vegetables are cooking, make the soufflé base. Melt the butter in a saucepan on the stovetop over medium heat. Add the flour, stir and cook for a minute or two. Add the paprika, nutmeg, salt and pepper. Whisk in the milk and bring the mixture to a simmer to thicken. Remove the pan from the heat and add the cheese, stirring to melt. Let the mixture cool for just a few minutes and then whisk the egg yolks in, one at a time. Stir in the cooked mushrooms and asparagus. Let this soufflé base cool.

5. In a separate bowl, whisk the egg whites to soft peak stage (the point at which the whites can almost stand up on the end of your whisk). Fold the whipped egg whites into the soufflé base, adding a little at a time.

6. Pre-heat the air fryer to 330°F.

7. Transfer the batter carefully to the buttered ramekins, leaving about ½-inch at the top. Place the ramekins into the air fryer basket and air-fry for 14 minutes. The soufflés should have risen nicely and be brown on top. Serve immediately.

The rule of thumb with soufflés is to have everyone sitting at the table ready to eat before the soufflés have finished cooking. It's inevitable that the soufflé will fall when it comes out of the air fryer, so in order for everyone to see it in all its glory...everyone waits for a soufflé because a soufflé waits for no-one!

Vegetables

Steak Fries

You can serve these with a delicious steak out of the air fryer, or on the side of a weekend breakfast plate. They are well seasoned on the outside and tender and moist on the inside.

Serves
4

Temperature
400°F

Cooking Time
18 to 20 minutes

2 russet potatoes, scrubbed and cut into wedges lengthwise

1 tablespoon olive oil

2 teaspoons seasoning salt (recipe below)

1. Pre-heat the air fryer to 400°F.

2. Toss the potatoes with the olive oil and the seasoning salt.

3. Air-fry for 18 to 20 minutes (depending on the size of the wedges), turning the potatoes over gently a few times throughout the cooking process to brown and cook them evenly.

 Substitution

You can also make steak fries with Montreal Steak Seasoning for an easy variation.

Seasoning Salt

1½ teaspoons kosher salt

½ teaspoon paprika

½ teaspoon freshly ground black pepper

⅛ teaspoon garlic powder

⅛ teaspoon onion powder

⅛ teaspoon sugar

1. Combine all ingredients.

2. Store in an airtight container indefinitely.

Roasted Brussels Sprouts with Bacon

I always feel like bacon is the secret weapon for Brussels sprouts. The two go so nicely together and a little bacon has convinced many a Brussels sprouts hater that the little member of the cabbage family is not so bad. 😊

Serves
4

Temperature
380°F

Cooking Time
5 + 15 minutes

4 slices thick-cut bacon, chopped (about ¼ pound)

1 pound Brussels sprouts, halved (or quartered if large)

freshly ground black pepper

1. Pre-heat the air fryer to 380ºF.

2. Air-fry the bacon for 5 minutes, shaking the basket once or twice during the cooking time.

3. Add the Brussels sprouts to the basket and drizzle a little bacon fat from the bottom of the air fryer drawer into the basket. Toss the sprouts to coat with the bacon fat. Air-fry for an additional 15 minutes, or until the Brussels sprouts are tender to a knifepoint.

4. Season with freshly ground black pepper.

Dress It Up

While I do love the simplicity of this recipe, you can take it to the next level by simply drizzling with a little aged balsamic vinegar (or balsamic reduction) at the end and tossing in some chopped fresh parsley.

Salt and Pepper Baked Potatoes

Quick, easy and crispy on the outside baked potatoes! Of course, because potatoes don't come in one size, you'll need to flex a little on the timing of this recipe. If your potatoes are very large, add a few minutes to the cooking time and test with a paring knife to make sure they are as tender as you like them.

Serves
4

Temperature
400°F

Cooking Time
40 minutes

1 to 2 tablespoons olive oil

4 medium russet potatoes
(about 9 to 10 ounces each)

salt and coarsely ground black pepper

butter, sour cream, chopped fresh chives,
scallions or bacon bits (optional)

1. Pre-heat the air fryer to 400°F.

2. Rub the olive oil all over the potatoes and season them generously with salt and coarsely ground black pepper. Pierce all sides of the potatoes several times with the tines of a fork.

3. Air-fry for 40 minutes, turning the potatoes over halfway through the cooking time.

4. Serve the potatoes, split open with butter, sour cream, fresh chives, scallions or bacon bits.

Dress It Up

Serve these potatoes fully loaded by splitting the finished potatoes open, filling with grated Cheddar cheese, bacon bits, and any other cooked topping that you would like. Then, pop them back into the air fryer for a few minutes at 350°F to melt the cheese.

Mini Hasselback Potatoes

Hasselback potatoes are baked potatoes dressed up for a night on the town! They originated at a Swedish restaurant called the Hasselbacken, and it didn't take cooks around the world long to start copying the pretty ingenious technique. Slicing the potatoes part way through and then baking them crisps the edges of the potato while keeping the center soft and fluffy. Delicious and elegant all at the same time!

Serves
4 to 5

Temperature
400°F

Cooking Time
25 minutes

1½ pounds baby Yukon Gold potatoes (about 10)

5 tablespoons butter, cut into very thin slices

salt and freshly ground black pepper

1 tablespoon vegetable oil

¼ cup grated Parmesan cheese (optional)

chopped fresh parsley or chives

1. Pre-heat the air fryer to 400°F.

2. Make six to eight deep vertical slits across the top of each potato about three quarters of the way down. Make sure the slits are deep enough to allow the slices to spread apart a little, but don't cut all the way through the potato. Place a thin slice of butter between each of the slices and season generously with salt and pepper.

3. Transfer the potatoes to the air fryer basket. Pack them in next to each other. It's alright if some of the potatoes sit on top or rest on another potato. Air-fry for 20 minutes.

4. Spray or brush the potatoes with a little vegetable oil and sprinkle the Parmesan cheese on top (if using). Air-fry for an additional 5 minutes. Garnish with chopped parsley or chives and serve hot.

Did You Know...?

To help slicing potatoes for this dish, you can buy a special Hasselback potato slicer. It looks a lot like a concave soap dish where the sides are higher than the middle, thereby preventing your knife from reaching the bottom of the potato. But if you can't find a Hasselback potato slicer, try using two chopsticks on your cutting board which will do the trick almost as well.

Rosemary Roasted Potatoes with Lemon

This quick and easy side dish will become a staple for you. It's truly the easiest way to get delicious potatoes on the table in minutes.

Serves
4

Temperature
400°F

Cooking Time
12 minutes

1 pound small red-skinned potatoes, halved or cut into bite-sized chunks

1 tablespoon olive oil

1 teaspoon finely chopped fresh rosemary

¼ teaspoon salt

freshly ground black pepper

1 tablespoon lemon zest

1. Pre-heat the air fryer to 400°F.

2. Toss the potatoes with the olive oil, rosemary, salt and freshly ground black pepper.

3. Air-fry for 12 minutes (depending on the size of the chunks), tossing the potatoes a few times throughout the cooking process.

4. As soon as the potatoes are tender to a knifepoint, toss them with the lemon zest and more salt if desired.

Substitution

You can use any herb you like for this easy side dish. Oregano with lemon is especially nice.

Dress It Up

Grating a little fresh Parmigiano-Reggiano cheese on top makes this even MORE delicious!

Parsnip Fries with Romesco Sauce

To be perfectly honest, while parsnip fries are a nice variation on potato fries, my favorite part of this recipe is the delicious dip that accompanies them. Romesco sauce is a roasted red pepper based sauce that is incredibly versatile, so is nice to have on hand. There are a few components to the sauce, which you make in the air fryer, but the good news is that this makes a lot of sauce, so you will have leftovers.

Serves

2

Temperature

400°F

Cooking Time

10 + 4 +10 minutes

Romesco Sauce:

1 red bell pepper, halved and seeded

1 (1-inch) thick slice of Italian bread, torn into pieces (about 1 to 1½ cups)

1 cup almonds, toasted

olive oil

½ Jalapeño pepper, seeded

1 tablespoon fresh parsley leaves

1 clove garlic

2 Roma tomatoes, peeled and seeded (or ⅓ cup canned crushed tomatoes)

1 tablespoon red wine vinegar

¼ teaspoon smoked paprika

½ teaspoon salt

¾ cup olive oil

3 parsnips, peeled and cut into long strips

2 teaspoons olive oil

salt and freshly ground black pepper

1. Pre-heat the air fryer to 400°F.

2. Place the red pepper halves, cut side down, in the air fryer basket and air-fry for 8 to 10 minutes, or until the skin turns black all over. Remove the pepper from the air fryer and let it cool. When it is cool enough to handle, peel the pepper.

3. Toss the torn bread and almonds with a little olive oil and air-fry for 4 minutes, shaking the basket a couple times throughout the cooking time. When the bread and almonds are nicely toasted, remove them from the air fryer and let them cool for just a minute or two.

4. Combine the toasted bread, almonds, roasted red pepper, Jalapeño pepper, parsley, garlic, tomatoes, vinegar, smoked paprika and salt in a food processor or blender. Process until smooth. With the processor running, add the olive oil through the feed tube until the sauce comes together in a smooth paste that is barely pourable.

5. Toss the parsnip strips with the olive oil, salt and freshly ground black pepper and air-fry at 400°F for 10 minutes, shaking the basket a couple times during the cooking process so they brown and cook evenly. Serve the parsnip fries warm with the Romesco sauce to dip into.

You could take out a step of this recipe by using store-bought roasted red pepper instead of roasting the pepper yourself. If you do roast the pepper yourself, covering the pepper with an inverted bowl while it cools will help to steam off the skin.

Roasted Herbed Shiitake Mushrooms

Mushrooms are such a versatile side dish or accompaniment. These are delicious with an air-fried rib-eye steak, a chicken breast or a fillet of halibut or sea bass.

Serves
4

Temperature
400°F

Cooking Time
5 minutes

8 ounces shiitake mushrooms, stems removed and caps roughly chopped

1 tablespoon olive oil

½ teaspoon salt

freshly ground black pepper

1 teaspoon chopped fresh thyme leaves

1 teaspoon chopped fresh oregano

1 tablespoon chopped fresh parsley

1. Pre-heat the air fryer to 400°F.

2. Toss the mushrooms with the olive oil, salt, pepper, thyme and oregano. Air-fry for 5 minutes, shaking the basket once or twice during the cooking process. The mushrooms will still be somewhat chewy with a meaty texture. If you'd like them a little more tender, add a couple of minutes to this cooking time.

3. Once cooked, add the parsley to the mushrooms and toss. Season again to taste and serve.

Did You Know...?

The stems of shiitake mushrooms are much tougher than the caps. They are edible, but rarely used. For this recipe, save the stems for a vegetable stock or just discard them.

Roasted Ratatouille Vegetables

This is a great late summer dish that can be served as a side dish, or dressed up into a meal by itself!

Serves
2 to 4

Temperature
400°F

Cooking Time
15 minutes

1 baby or Japanese eggplant, cut into 1½-inch cubes

1 red pepper, cut into 1-inch chunks

1 yellow pepper, cut into 1-inch chunks

1 zucchini, cut into 1-inch chunks

1 clove garlic, minced

½ teaspoon dried basil

1 tablespoon olive oil

salt and freshly ground black pepper

¼ cup sliced sun-dried tomatoes in oil

2 tablespoons chopped fresh basil

1. Pre-heat the air fryer to 400°F.

2. Toss the eggplant, peppers and zucchini with the garlic, dried basil, olive oil, salt and freshly ground black pepper.

3. Air-fry the vegetables at 400°F for 15 minutes, shaking the basket a few times during the cooking process to redistribute the ingredients.

4. As soon as the vegetables are tender, toss them with the sliced sun-dried tomatoes and fresh basil and serve.

Dress It Up

These vegetables are delicious over pasta with a little extra virgin olive oil, thrown onto a pizza or even added to a marinara.

Florentine Stuffed Tomatoes

This makes a very sweet little vegetable side dish next to some chicken, fish or steak, but can also be served on it's own as a vegetarian entrée or a light lunch.

Serves
2 to 4

Temperature
350°F

Cooking Time
12 minutes per batch

1 cup frozen spinach,
thawed and squeezed dry

¼ cup toasted pine nuts

¼ cup grated mozzarella cheese

½ cup crumbled feta cheese

½ cup coarse fresh breadcrumbs

1 tablespoon olive oil

salt and freshly ground black pepper

2 to 3 beefsteak tomatoes, halved
horizontally and insides scooped out

1. Combine the spinach, pine nuts, mozzarella and feta cheeses, breadcrumbs, olive oil, salt and freshly ground black pepper in a bowl. Spoon the mixture into the tomato halves. You should have enough filling for 2 to 3 tomatoes, depending on how big they are.

2. Pre-heat the air fryer to 350°F.

3. Place three or four tomato halves (depending on whether you're using 2 or 3 tomatoes and how big they are) into the air fryer and air-fry for 12 minutes. The tomatoes should be soft but still manageable and the tops should be lightly browned. Repeat with second batch if necessary.

4. Let the tomatoes cool for just a minute or two before serving.

Did You Know...?

The air fryer is perfect for toasting nuts. Air-fry the pine nuts for this recipe for just 2 minutes at 370°F before adding to the filling mixture. If some of the pine nuts fall through the holes in the basket, no problem. Just remove them from the bottom drawer.

Sesame Carrots and Sugar Snap Peas

Looking for an interesting vegetable side dish that will add a little color to your plate? Look no further!

Serves
4

Temperature
360°F/400°F

Cooking Time
16 minutes

1 pound carrots, peeled
sliced on the bias (½-inch slices)

1 teaspoon olive oil

salt and freshly ground black pepper

⅓ cup honey

1 tablespoon sesame oil

1 tablespoon soy sauce

½ teaspoon minced fresh ginger

4 ounces sugar snap peas (about 1 cup)

1½ teaspoons sesame seeds

1. Pre-heat the air fryer to 360°F.

2. Toss the carrots with the olive oil, season with salt and pepper and air-fry for 10 minutes, shaking the basket once or twice during the cooking process.

3. Combine the honey, sesame oil, soy sauce and minced ginger in a large bowl. Add the sugar snap peas and the air-fried carrots to the honey mixture, toss to coat and return everything to the air fryer basket.

4. Turn up the temperature to 400°F and air-fry for an additional 6 minutes, shaking the basket once during the cooking process.

5. Transfer the carrots and sugar snap peas to a serving bowl. Pour the sauce from the bottom of the cooker over the vegetables and sprinkle sesame seeds over top. Serve immediately.

Did You Know...?

Regular sesame oil (called for in this recipe) has a very high smoke point, making it a great oil to use in the air fryer. It can turn rancid relatively easily, however, so store it in your refrigerator for longer life. Toasted sesame oil is visibly different from regular sesame oil (very dark in color) and imparts a very strong flavor. You can use a few drops of toasted sesame oil at the end of this recipe if you want a stronger sesame flavor.

Spicy Fried Green Beans

Need a quick side dish with a little kick? Here's the answer!

Serves
2 to 4

Temperature
400°F

Cooking Time
6 to 8 minutes

12 ounces green beans, trimmed

2 small dried hot red chili peppers (like árbol)

¼ cup panko breadcrumbs

1 tablespoon olive oil

½ teaspoon salt

⅛ teaspoon crushed red pepper flakes

2 scallions, thinly sliced

1. Pre-heat the air fryer to 400°F.

2. Toss the green beans, chili peppers and panko breadcrumbs with the olive oil, salt and crushed red pepper flakes.

3. Air-fry for 6 to 8 minutes (depending on the size of the beans), shaking the basket once during the cooking process. The crumbs will fall into the bottom drawer – don't worry.

4. Transfer the green beans to a serving dish, sprinkle the scallions and the toasted crumbs from the air fryer drawer on top and serve. The dried peppers are not to be eaten, but they do look nice with the green beans. You can leave them in, or take them out as you please.

If you happen to have some Sichuan peppercorns, you can use that instead of the crushed red pepper flakes for a more authentically Chinese (and somewhat mouth-numbing) flavor.

Fried Cauliflower
with Parmesan Lemon Dressing

You'll see that this recipe calls for Parmigiano-Reggiano cheese, rather than just calling for Parmesan. That's because the quality of the cheese plays such an important role in this recipe. Splurge on a wedge of true aged Parmigiano-Reggiano and grate it yourself for this dressing. You won't regret it and a little will go a long way.

Serves
2 to 4

Temperature
400°F

Cooking Time
12 minutes

4 cups cauliflower florets
(about half a large head)

1 tablespoon olive oil

salt and freshly ground black pepper

1 teaspoon finely chopped lemon zest

1 tablespoon fresh lemon juice
(about half a lemon)

¼ cup grated Parmigiano-Reggiano
cheese

4 tablespoons extra virgin olive oil

¼ teaspoon salt

lots of freshly ground black pepper

1 tablespoon chopped fresh parsley

1. Pre-heat the air fryer to 400ºF.

2. Toss the cauliflower florets with the olive oil, salt and freshly ground black pepper. Air-fry for 12 minutes, shaking the basket a couple of times during the cooking process.

3. While the cauliflower is frying, make the dressing. Combine the lemon zest, lemon juice, Parmigiano-Reggiano cheese and olive oil in a small bowl. Season with salt and lots of freshly ground black pepper. Stir in the parsley.

4. Turn the fried cauliflower out onto a serving platter and drizzle the dressing over the top.

Dress It Up

Toss this cauliflower with arugula and tomatoes before dressing with the lemon-Parmesan dressing for a delicious salad.

Substitution

This recipe also works really nicely with broccoli. The tiny floral shoots of the broccoli florets get a little darker and crispier than the rest, giving the vegetable interesting textures.

Fried Eggplant Balls

There's no more graceful title for this dish – though I wish there was! These balls formed out of cooked eggplant, cheese, breadcrumbs and herbs make a great appetizer, snack, or an interesting vegetarian substitute for meatballs!

Serves
4

Temperature
400°F/350°F

Cooking Time
25 + 15 minutes

1 medium eggplant (about 1 pound)

olive oil

salt and freshly ground black pepper

1 cup grated Parmesan cheese

2 cups fresh breadcrumbs

2 tablespoons chopped fresh parsley

2 tablespoons chopped fresh basil

1 clove garlic, minced

1 egg, lightly beaten

½ cup fine dried breadcrumbs

1. Pre-heat the air fryer to 400ºF.

2. Quarter the eggplant by cutting it in half both lengthwise and horizontally. Make a few slashes in the flesh of the eggplant but not through the skin. Brush the cut surface of the eggplant generously with olive oil and transfer to the air fryer basket, cut side up. Air-fry for 10 minutes. Turn the eggplant quarters cut side down and air-fry for another 15 minutes or until the eggplant is soft all the way through. You may need to rotate the pieces in the air fryer so that they cook evenly. Transfer the eggplant to a cutting board to cool.

3. Place the Parmesan cheese, the fresh breadcrumbs, fresh herbs, garlic and egg in a food processor. Scoop the flesh out of the eggplant, discarding the skin and any pieces that are tough. You should have about 1 to 1½ cups of eggplant. Add the eggplant to the food processor and process everything together until smooth. Season with salt and pepper. Refrigerate the mixture for at least 30 minutes.

4. Place the dried breadcrumbs into a shallow dish or onto a plate. Scoop heaping tablespoons of the eggplant mixture into the dried breadcrumbs. Roll the dollops of eggplant in the bread-crumbs and then shape into small balls. You should have 16 to 18 eggplant balls at the end. Refrigerate until you are ready to air-fry.

5. Pre-heat the air fryer to 350ºF.

6. Spray the eggplant balls and the air fryer basket with olive oil. Air-fry the eggplant balls for 15 minutes, rotating the balls during the cooking process to brown evenly.

Dress It Up

Serve these eggplant balls with pasta and marinara for a main meal, or as an appetizer with a dip like the cucumber-yogurt dip on page 120.

Fried Pearl Onions
with Balsamic Vinegar and Basil

Roasting onions in their whole form results in a sweet and tender addition to any meal. I love these onions tossed in with potatoes and roasted together, but they are fantastic added to pasta or slipped into a sandwich too.

Serves
2 to 4

Temperature
400°F

Cooking Time
10 minutes

1 pound fresh pearl onions

1 tablespoon olive oil

salt and freshly ground black pepper

1 teaspoon high quality aged balsamic vinegar

1 tablespoon chopped fresh basil leaves (or mint)

1. Pre-heat the air fryer to 400°F.

2. Decide whether you want to peel the onions before or after they cook. Peeling them ahead of time is a little more laborious. Peeling after they cook is easier, but a little messier since the onions are hot and you may discard more of the onion than you'd like to. If you opt to peel them first, trim the tiny root of the onions off and pinch off any loose papery skins. (It's ok if there are some skins left on the onions.) Toss the pearl onions with the olive oil, salt and freshly ground black pepper.

3. Air-fry for 10 minutes, shaking the basket a couple of times during the cooking process. (If your pearl onions are very large, you may need to add a couple of minutes to this cooking time.)

4. Let the onions cool slightly and then slip off any remaining skins.

5. Toss the onions with the balsamic vinegar and basil and serve.

 Dress It Up

You can really make these onions a part of a great side dish. Toss them with any combination of other roasted vegetables, or add a little sun-dried tomato and sun-dried tomato oil for a delicious variation to the above.

Substitution

This is actually a non-substitute tip! Don't try this with frozen pearl onions. They are just too moist to get the results we're looking for.

Roasted Garlic and Thyme Tomatoes

These tomatoes are great on their own, but also make a great ingredient for other meals. They are wonderful in pasta, a sandwich, a salad, on a crostini or pizza… or just a fork! So many options!

Serves
2 to 4

Temperature
390°F

Cooking Time
15 minutes

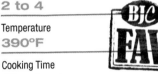

4 Roma tomatoes

1 tablespoon olive oil

salt and freshly ground black pepper

1 clove garlic, minced

½ teaspoon dried thyme

1. Pre-heat the air fryer to 390ºF.

2. Cut the tomatoes in half and scoop out the seeds and any pithy parts with your fingers. Place the tomatoes in a bowl and toss with the olive oil, salt, pepper, garlic and thyme.

3. Transfer the tomatoes to the air fryer, cut side up. Air-fry for 15 minutes. The edges should just start to brown. Let the tomatoes cool to an edible temperature for a few minutes and then use in pastas, on top of crostini, or as an accompaniment to any poultry, meat or fish.

Dress It Up

A stack of these tomatoes will be the star of the plate when arranged on an antipasto platter. The air fryer is a great way to make all sorts of antipasti. You can roast your own peppers, mushrooms and artichokes and then marinate them to build the supporting cast.

Desserts

Chocolate Soufflés

Soufflés are always impressive and despite what you may think, are very easy to make. In addition, even after they fall (and every soufflé will fall), they are delicious. The good news is that you can make these ahead of time – even a full day ahead of time! Put the batter in the ramekins and store them, covered with plastic wrap, in the refrigerator. Pop them into the pre-heated air fryer as you sit down for dinner and you'll have dessert on the table in 14 minutes – plenty of time to eat and clear the table.

Serves
2

Temperature
330°F

Cooking Time
14 minutes

butter and sugar for greasing the ramekins

3 ounces semi-sweet chocolate, chopped

¼ cup unsalted butter

2 eggs, yolks and white separated

3 tablespoons sugar

½ teaspoon pure vanilla extract

2 tablespoons all-purpose flour

powdered sugar, for dusting the finished soufflés

heavy cream, for serving

1. Butter and sugar two 6-ounce ramekins. (Butter the ramekins and then coat the butter with sugar by shaking it around in the ramekin and dumping out any excess.)

2. Melt the chocolate and butter together, either in the microwave or in a double boiler. In a separate bowl, beat the egg yolks vigorously. Add the sugar and the vanilla extract and beat well again. Drizzle in the chocolate and butter, mixing well. Stir in the flour, combining until there are no lumps.

3. Pre-heat the air fryer to 330°F.

4. In a separate bowl, whisk the egg whites to soft peak stage (the point at which the whites can almost stand up on the end of your whisk). Fold the whipped egg whites into the chocolate mixture gently and in stages.

5. Transfer the batter carefully to the buttered ramekins, leaving about ½-inch at the top. (You may have a little extra batter, depending on how airy the batter is, so you might be able to squeeze out a third soufflé if you want to.) Place the ramekins into the air fryer basket and air-fry for 14 minutes. The soufflés should have risen nicely and be brown on top. (Don't worry if the top gets a little dark – you'll be covering it with powdered sugar in the next step.)

6. Dust with powdered sugar and serve immediately with heavy cream to pour over the top at the table.

Did You Know...?

When you whip egg whites, the bowl and the whisk need to be super clean, with no fat on them at all, in order for the whites to whip up; so, wash your whisk carefully after you beat the egg yolks.

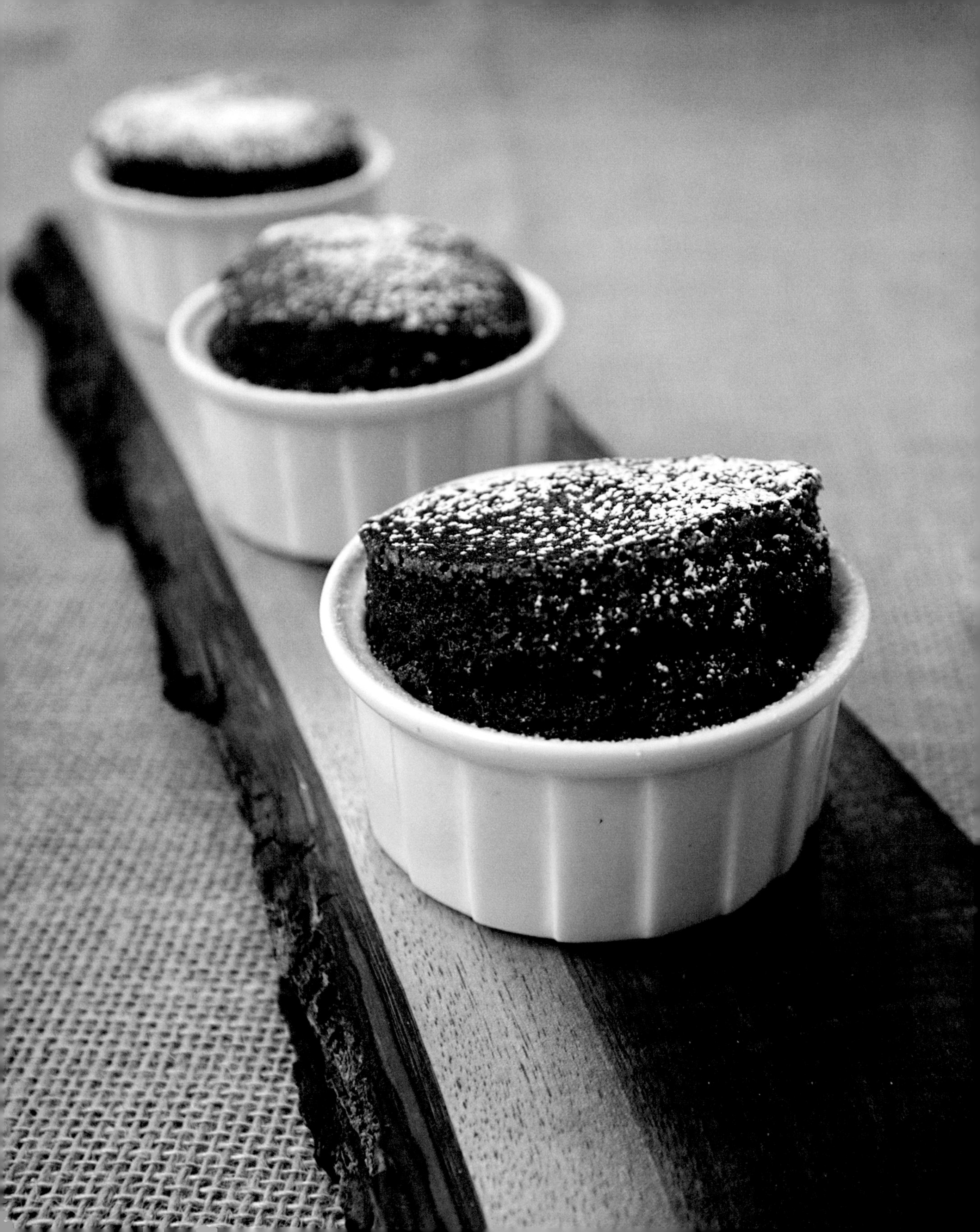

Boston Cream Donut Holes

My friend Lisa's favorite donuts are Boston Cream filled balls of heaven. She perfected this recipe and now we're sharing it with you! Of course, you can fill the donuts with jam instead of custard, or simply roll the donuts in powdered sugar, cinnamon sugar, or dip in chocolate with sprinkles if you don't want to fill them. Donuts do take a little work in the form of time, but they are easy to make and just look at the result! Look quickly, because they won't last long!

Serves
24 donut holes

Temperature
400°F

Cooking Time
12 minutes
(4 minutes per batch)

1½ cups bread flour

1 teaspoon active dry yeast

1 tablespoon sugar

¼ teaspoon salt

½ cup warm milk

½ teaspoon pure vanilla extract

2 egg yolks

2 tablespoons butter, melted

vegetable oil

Custard Filling:

1 (3.4-ounce) box French vanilla instant pudding mix

¾ cup whole milk

¼ cup heavy cream

Chocolate Glaze:

1 cup chocolate chips

⅓ cup heavy cream

1. Combine the flour, yeast, sugar and salt in the bowl of a stand mixer. Add the milk, vanilla, egg yolks and butter. Mix until the dough starts to come together in a ball. Transfer the dough to a floured surface and knead the dough by hand for 2 minutes. Shape the dough into a ball, place it in a large oiled bowl, cover the bowl with a clean kitchen towel and let the dough rise for 1 to 1½ hours or until the dough has doubled in size.

2. When the dough has risen, punch it down and roll it into a 24-inch log. Cut the dough into 24 pieces and roll each piece into a ball. Place the dough balls on a baking sheet and let them rise for another 30 minutes.

3. Pre-heat the air fryer to 400°F.

4. Spray or brush the dough balls lightly with vegetable oil and air-fry eight at a time for 4 minutes, turning them over halfway through the cooking time.

5. While donut holes are cooking, make the filling and chocolate glaze. To make the filling, use an electric hand mixer to beat the French vanilla pudding, milk and ¼ cup of heavy cream together for 2 minutes.

6. To make the chocolate glaze, place the chocolate chips in a medium-sized bowl. Bring the heavy cream to a boil on the stovetop and pour it over the chocolate chips. Stir until the chips are melted and the glaze is smooth.

7. To fill the donut holes, place the custard filling in a pastry bag with a long tip. Poke a hole into the side of the donut hole with a small knife. Wiggle the knife around to make room for the filling. Place the pastry bag tip into the hole and slowly squeeze the custard into the center of the donut. Dip the top half of the donut into the chocolate glaze, letting any excess glaze drip back into the bowl. Let the glazed donut holes sit for a few minutes before serving.

Bananas Foster Bread Pudding

Oh boy... this one is a head slapper! Bananas Foster is a classic dessert made with bananas, butter, sugar and rum that is flambéed before serving over vanilla ice cream. This recipe takes a shortcut by using store-bought caramel sauce and leaving out the rum. While this is obviously a dessert, it has been enjoyed in my house for breakfast, but that's a secret!

Serves
4

Temperature
350°F

Cooking Time
50 minutes
(25 minutes per batch)

½ cup brown sugar

3 eggs

¾ cup half and half

1 teaspoon pure vanilla extract

6 cups cubed Kings Hawaiian bread (½-inch cubes), ½ pound

2 bananas, sliced

1 cup caramel sauce, plus more for serving

1. Pre-heat the air fryer to 350°F.

2. Combine the brown sugar, eggs, half and half and vanilla extract in a large bowl, whisking until the sugar has dissolved and the mixture is smooth. Stir in the cubed bread and toss to coat all the cubes evenly. Let the bread sit for 10 minutes to absorb the liquid.

3. Mix the sliced bananas and caramel sauce together in a separate bowl.

4. Fill the bottom of 4 (8-ounce) greased ramekins with half the bread cubes. Divide the caramel and bananas between the ramekins, spooning them on top of the bread cubes. Top with the remaining bread cubes and wrap each ramekin with aluminum foil, tenting the foil at the top to leave some room for the bread to puff up during the cooking process.

5. Air-fry two bread puddings at a time for 25 minutes. Let the puddings cool a little and serve warm with additional caramel sauce drizzled on top. A scoop of vanilla ice cream would be nice too and in keeping with our Bananas Foster theme!

Kings Hawaiian bread is a brand of sweet Hawaiian bread made with butter and eggs. It is tasty, tender and moist and makes a great bread pudding. It's quite widely distributed across the United States, but if you can't find it, substitute an egg-based bread like brioche or challah.

Caramel Apple Crumble

The trickiest part of this recipe is finding the ceramic baking dish to bake it in! Once you have the baking dish, the rest is a breeze. Put it all together and pop it into the air fryer before you start preparing your dinner. By the time you've finished dinner and are ready for dessert, just pull out the ice cream and enjoy!

Serves
6 to 8

Temperature
330°F

Cooking Time
50 minutes

4 apples, peeled and thinly sliced

2 tablespoons sugar

1 tablespoon flour

1 teaspoon ground cinnamon

¼ teaspoon ground allspice

healthy pinch ground nutmeg

10 caramel squares,
cut into small pieces

Crumble Topping:

¾ cup rolled oats

¼ cup sugar

⅓ cup flour

¼ teaspoon ground cinnamon

6 tablespoons butter, melted

1. Pre-heat the air fryer to 330°F.

2. Combine the apples, sugar, flour, and spices in a large bowl and toss to coat. Add the caramel pieces and mix well. Pour the apple mixture into a 1-quart round baking dish that will fit in your air fryer basket (6-inch diameter).

3. To make the crumble topping, combine the rolled oats, sugar, flour and cinnamon in a small bowl. Add the melted butter and mix well. Top the apples with the crumble mixture. Cover the entire dish with aluminum foil and transfer the dish to the air fryer basket, lowering the dish into the basket using a sling made of aluminum foil (fold a piece of aluminum foil into a strip about 2-inches wide by 24-inches long). Fold the ends of the aluminum foil over the top of the dish before returning the basket to the air fryer.

4. Air-fry at 330°F for 25 minutes. Remove the aluminum foil and continue to air-fry for another 25 minutes. Serve the crumble warm with whipped cream or vanilla ice cream, if desired.

The best apples for baking are those with a sweet-tart flavor that can keep their shape under high-heat conditions and not turn to mush. My favorite baking apples tend to also be my favorite eating apples, so I'm in luck! Cripps Pink (Pink Lady), Honeycrisp and Gala are all good choices.

Puff Pastry Apples

These delicious and cute apple desserts are the perfect size for a single serving and are much faster to make than a whole pie. Serve them with some vanilla ice cream drizzled with caramel syrup and you will have nothing left but empty plates!

Serves
4

Temperature
350°F

Cooking Time
10 minutes

BJC
FAV

3 Rome or Gala apples, peeled

2 tablespoons sugar

1 teaspoon all-purpose flour

1 teaspoon ground cinnamon

⅛ teaspoon ground ginger

pinch ground nutmeg

1 sheet puff pastry

1 tablespoon butter, cut into 4 pieces

1 egg, beaten

vegetable oil

vanilla ice cream (optional)

caramel sauce (optional)

BLUE JEAN
Chef
Did You Know...?

If you're making these for a dinner party and want to save yourself the last minute work, you can make these apples ahead of time on the same day you are serving them, and then re-heat them in the air fryer at 300°F for 3 minutes.

1. Remove the core from the apple by cutting the four sides off the apple around the core. Slice the pieces of apple into thin half-moons, about ¼-inch thick. Combine the sugar, flour, cinnamon, ginger, and nutmeg in a large bowl. Add the apples to the bowl and gently toss until the apples are evenly coated with the spice mixture. Set aside.

2. Cut the puff pastry sheet into a 12-inch by 12-inch square. Then quarter the sheet into four 6-inch squares. Save any remaining pastry for decorating the apples at the end.

3. Divide the spiced apples between the four puff pastry squares, stacking the apples in the center of each square and placing them flat on top of each other in a circle. Top the apples with a piece of the butter.

4. Brush the four edges of the pastry with the egg wash. Bring the four corners of the pastry together, wrapping them around the apple slices and pinching them together at the top in the style of a "beggars purse" appetizer. Fold the ends of the pastry corners down onto the apple making them look like leaves. Brush the entire apple with the egg wash.

5. Using the leftover dough, make leaves to decorate the apples. Cut out 8 leaf shapes, about 1½-inches long, "drawing" the leaf veins on the pastry leaves with a paring knife. Place 2 leaves on the top of each apple, tucking the ends of the leaves under the pastry in the center of the apples. Brush the top of the leaves with additional egg wash. Sprinkle the entire apple with some granulated sugar.

6. Pre-heat the air fryer to 350°F.

7. Spray or brush the inside of the air fryer basket with oil. Place the apples in the basket and air-fry for 6 minutes. Carefully turn the apples over – it's easiest to remove one apple, then flip the others over and finally return the last apple to the air fryer. Air-fry for an additional 4 minutes.

8. Serve the puff pastry apples warm with vanilla ice cream and drizzle with some caramel sauce.

Molten Chocolate Almond Cakes

The timing on these little cakes can be a little tricky, so pay attention to the cooking and cooling times listed below. Of course, even if the molten center is not soft enough, or even a little too soft, these decadent little desserts taste just as delicious and you won't have any disappointed eaters. That's the beauty of chocolate.

Serves
3

Temperature
330°F

Cooking Time
13 minutes

butter and flour for the ramekins

4 ounces bittersweet chocolate, chopped

½ cup (1 stick) unsalted butter

2 eggs

2 egg yolks

¼ cup sugar

½ teaspoon pure vanilla extract, or almond extract

1 tablespoon all-purpose flour

3 tablespoons ground almonds

8 to 12 semisweet chocolate discs (or 4 chunks of chocolate)

cocoa powder or powdered sugar, for dusting

toasted almonds, coarsely chopped

1. Butter and flour three (6-ounce) ramekins. (Butter the ramekins and then coat the butter with flour by shaking it around in the ramekin and dumping out any excess.)

2. Melt the chocolate and butter together, either in the microwave or in a double boiler. In a separate bowl, beat the eggs, egg yolks and sugar together until light and smooth. Add the vanilla extract. Whisk the chocolate mixture into the egg mixture. Stir in the flour and ground almonds.

3. Pre-heat the air fryer to 330°F.

4. Transfer the batter carefully to the buttered ramekins, filling halfway. Place two or three chocolate discs in the center of the batter and then fill the ramekins to ½-inch below the top with the remaining batter. Place the ramekins into the air fryer basket and air-fry at 330°F for 13 minutes. The sides of the cake should be set, but the centers should be slightly soft. Remove the ramekins from the air fryer and let the cakes sit for 5 minutes. (If you'd like the cake a little less molten, air-fry for 14 minutes and let the cakes sit for 4 minutes.)

5. Run a butter knife around the edge of the ramekins and invert the cakes onto a plate. Lift the ramekin off the plate slowly and carefully so that the cake doesn't break. Dust with cocoa powder or powdered sugar and serve with a scoop of ice cream and some coarsely chopped toasted almonds.

Did You Know...?

You can use a mini chopper or food processor to grind the almonds, but you could also use a coffee bean grinder. No need to clean the grinder out first – a little taste of coffee would be delicious in these cakes.

Mixed Berry Hand Pies

Who doesn't love a pie that you can hold in your hand?
That's right – no-one!
Get your hands busy!

Serves
4

Temperature
370°F

Cooking Time
30 minutes
(15 minutes per batch)

¾ cup sugar

½ teaspoon ground cinnamon

1 tablespoon cornstarch

1 cup blueberries

1 cup blackberries

1 cup raspberries, divided

1 teaspoon water

1 package refrigerated pie dough
(or your own homemade pie dough)

1 egg, beaten

1. Combine the sugar, cinnamon, and cornstarch in a small saucepan. Add the blueberries, blackberries, and ½ cup of the raspberries. Toss the berries gently to coat them evenly. Add the teaspoon of water to the saucepan and turn the stovetop on to medium-high heat, stirring occasionally. Once the berries break down, release their juice and start to simmer (about 5 minutes), simmer for another couple of minutes and then transfer the mixture to a bowl, stir in the remaining ½ cup of raspberries and let it cool.

2. Pre-heat the air fryer to 370°F.

3. Cut the pie dough into four 5-inch circles and four 6-inch circles.

4. Spread the 6-inch circles on a flat surface. Divide the berry filling between all four circles. Brush the perimeter of the dough circles with a little water. Place the 5-inch circles on top of the filling and press the perimeter of the dough circles together to seal. Roll the edges of the bottom circle up over the top circle to make a crust around the filling. Press a fork around the crust to make decorative indentations and to seal the crust shut. Brush the pies with egg wash and sprinkle a little sugar on top. Poke a small hole in the center of each pie with a paring knife to vent the dough.

5. Air-fry two pies at a time. Brush or spray the air fryer basket with oil and place the pies into the basket. Air-fry for 9 minutes. Turn the pies over and air-fry for another 6 minutes. Serve warm or at room temperature.

Did You Know...?

Turbinado or demerara sugar are sugars with larger crystals. They would be perfect to sprinkle on top of the hand pies before baking.

Carrot Cake with Cream Cheese Icing

I usually go for the chocolate desserts, but there's something about carrot cake that draws me in every time. I'm especially fond of cream cheese icing, so in this recipe there's enough icing to slice the cake in half horizontally and build a layer cake with icing in between the layers, or to simply spread thick icing on both the top and sides of the cake. Yum!

Serves
6 to 8

Temperature
350°F

Cooking Time
55 minutes

1¼ cups all-purpose flour

1 teaspoon baking powder

½ teaspoon baking soda

1 teaspoon ground cinnamon

¼ teaspoon ground nutmeg

¼ teaspoon salt

2 cups grated carrot
(about 3 to 4 medium carrots or 2 large)

¾ cup granulated sugar

¼ cup brown sugar

2 eggs

¾ cup canola or vegetable oil

For the icing:

8 ounces cream cheese,
softened at room temperature

8 tablespoons butter
(4 ounces or 1 stick),
softened at room temperature

1 cup powdered sugar

1 teaspoon pure vanilla extract

1. Grease a 7-inch cake pan.

2. Combine the flour, baking powder, baking soda, cinnamon, nutmeg and salt in a bowl. Add the grated carrots and toss well. In a separate bowl, beat the sugars and eggs together until light and frothy. Drizzle in the oil, beating constantly. Fold the egg mixture into the dry ingredients until everything is just combined and you no longer see any traces of flour. Pour the batter into the cake pan and wrap the pan completely in greased aluminum foil.

3. Pre-heat the air fryer to 350°F.

4. Lower the cake pan into the air fryer basket using a sling made of aluminum foil (fold a piece of aluminum foil into a strip about 2-inches wide by 24-inches long). Fold the ends of the aluminum foil into the air fryer, letting them rest on top of the cake. Air-fry for 40 minutes. Remove the aluminum foil cover and air-fry for an additional 15 minutes or until a skewer inserted into the center of the cake comes out clean and the top is nicely browned.

5. While the cake is cooking, beat the cream cheese, butter, powdered sugar and vanilla extract together using a hand mixer, stand mixer or food processor (or a lot of elbow grease!).

6. Remove the cake pan from the air fryer and let the cake cool in the cake pan for 10 minutes or so. Then remove the cake from the pan and let it continue to cool completely. Frost the cake with the cream cheese icing and serve.

Shortcut

The fastest way to make this cake is to use a food processor. Use the grating blades to grate the carrots and then transfer them to the dry ingredient bowl. No need to clean the bowl, just go right ahead and use the regular blade in the food processor to whip up the wet ingredients, drizzling in the oil.

Fried Banana S'mores

This is a dessert that I usually make on an outdoor grill, but it's perfect for the air fryer, where the basket can hold the bananas upright and keep them from tipping over. It delivers all the flavors of s'mores but with peanut butter and bananas thrown in. Plus, it's pretty fun to eat. Just hand the kids a spoon and get out of the way!

Serves
4

Temperature
400°F

Cooking Time
6 minutes

4 bananas

3 tablespoons mini semi-sweet chocolate chips

3 tablespoons mini peanut butter chips

3 tablespoons mini marshmallows

3 tablespoons graham cracker cereal

1. Pre-heat the air fryer to 400°F.

2. Slice into the un-peeled bananas lengthwise along the inside of the curve, but do not slice through the bottom of the peel. Open the banana slightly to form a pocket.

3. Fill each pocket with chocolate chips, peanut butter chips and marshmallows. Poke the graham cracker cereal into the filling.

4. Place the bananas in the air fryer basket, resting them on the side of the basket and each other to keep them upright with the filling facing up. Air-fry for 6 minutes, or until the bananas are soft to the touch, the peels have blackened and the chocolate and marshmallows have melted and toasted.

5. Let them cool for a couple of minutes and then simply serve with a spoon to scoop out the filling.

Did You Know...?

So many recipes require your bananas to be perfectly ripe. Here's one where you can get away with slightly under-ripe bananas. The heat from the air fryer softens the banana up and the other ingredients will compensate for a banana that is not overly sweet.

Glazed Cherry Turnovers

The beautiful thing about this recipe is that you can use any flavor of pie filing. Craving apple turnovers? No problem! Blueberry? Just pick up the best-quality can of the pie filling of your choice. Easy peasy!

Serves
8

Temperature
370°F

Cooking Time
56 minutes
(14 minutes per batch)

2 sheets frozen puff pastry, thawed

1 (21-ounce) can premium cherry pie filling

2 teaspoons ground cinnamon

1 egg, beaten

1 cup sliced almonds

1 cup powdered sugar

2 tablespoons milk

1. Roll a sheet of puff pastry out into a square that is approximately 10-inches by 10-inches. Cut this large square into quarters.

2. Mix the cherry pie filling and cinnamon together in a bowl. Spoon ¼ cup of the cherry filling into the center of each puff pastry square. Brush the perimeter of the pastry square with the egg wash. Fold one corner of the puff pastry over the cherry pie filling towards the opposite corner, forming a triangle. Seal the two edges of the pastry together with the tip of a fork, making a design with the tines. Brush the top of the turnovers with the egg wash and sprinkle sliced almonds over each one. Repeat these steps with the second sheet of puff pastry. You should have eight turnovers at the end.

3. Pre-heat the air fryer to 370°F.

4. Air-fry two turnovers at a time for 14 minutes, carefully turning them over halfway through the cooking time.

5. While the turnovers are cooking, make the glaze by whisking the powdered sugar and milk together in a small bowl until smooth. Let the glaze sit for a minute so the sugar can absorb the milk. If the consistency is still too thick to drizzle, add a little more milk, a drop at a time, and stir until smooth.

6. Let the cooked cherry turnovers sit for at least 10 minutes. Then drizzle the glaze over each turnover in a zigzag motion. Serve warm or at room temperature.

Shortcut

The shortcut for this dessert already exists in the recipe – using store-bought pie filling and store-bought puff pastry. Because there are so few ingredients in this recipe, make sure those ingredients are of the best quality. Pick up the best premium pie filling you can find.

Orange Gooey Butter Cake

This is a take on the classic recipe for gooey butter cake from St. Louis, which in reality is more like a bar than a cake. This recipe is all about the butter! So, be sure to use a good quality European style butter, which has more butterfat and a creamier taste.

Serves
6 to 8

Temperature
350°F

Cooking Time
8 + 77 minutes

Crust Layer:

½ cup flour

¼ cup sugar

½ teaspoon baking powder

⅛ teaspoon salt

2 ounces (½ stick) unsalted European style butter, melted

1 egg

1 teaspoon orange extract

2 tablespoons orange zest

Gooey Butter Layer:

8 ounces cream cheese, softened

4 ounces (1 stick) unsalted European style butter, melted

2 eggs

2 teaspoons orange extract

2 tablespoons orange zest

4 cups powdered sugar

Garnish:

powdered sugar

orange slices

1. Pre-heat the air fryer to 350°F.

2. Grease a 7-inch cake pan and line the bottom with parchment paper. Combine the flour, sugar, baking powder and salt in a bowl. Add the melted butter, egg, orange extract and orange zest. Mix well and press this mixture into the bottom of the greased cake pan. Lower the pan into the basket using an aluminum foil sling (fold a piece of aluminum foil into a strip about 2-inches wide by 24-inches long). Fold the ends of the aluminum foil over the top of the dish before returning the basket to the air fryer. Air-fry uncovered for 8 minutes.

3. To make the gooey butter layer, beat the cream cheese, melted butter, eggs, orange extract and orange zest in a large bowl using an electric hand mixer. Add the powdered sugar in stages, beat until smooth with each addition. Pour this mixture on top of the baked crust in the cake pan. Wrap the pan with a piece of greased aluminum foil, tenting the top of the foil to leave a little room for the cake to rise.

4. Air-fry for 60 minutes at 350°F. Remove the aluminum foil and air-fry for an additional 17 minutes.

5. Let the cake cool inside the pan for at least 10 minutes. Then, run a butter knife around the cake and let the cake cool completely in the pan. When cooled, run the butter knife around the edges of the cake again and invert it onto a plate and then back onto a serving platter. Sprinkle the powdered sugar over the top of the cake and garnish with orange slices.

Did You Know...?

If you have any trouble removing the cake from the pan, bring a sauté pan of water to a boil on the stovetop. Dip the pan into the boiling water for 10 seconds and then invert it. It will pop right out.

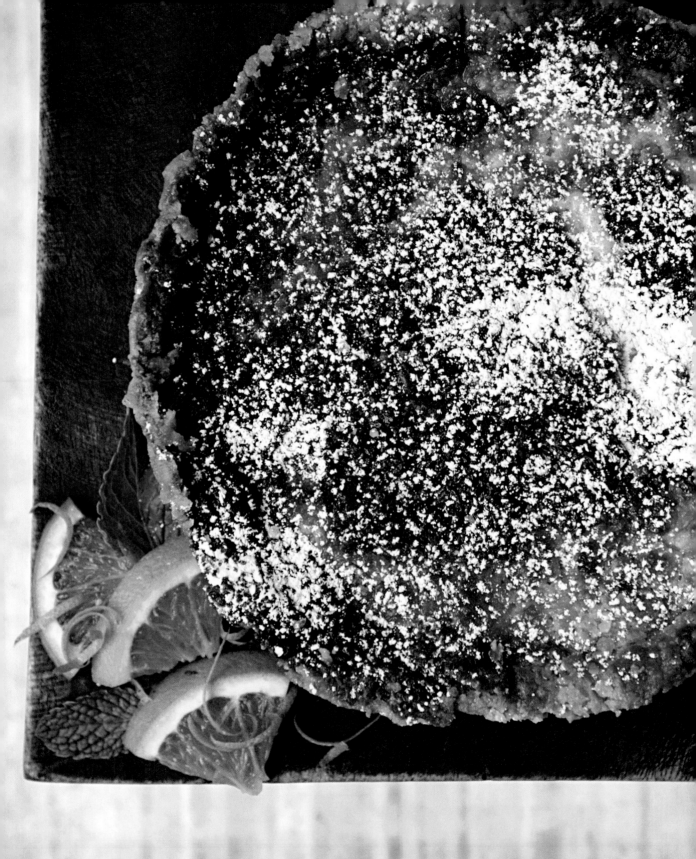

Nutella® Torte

This torte should be gooey in the center, but chewy on the sides. It's decadent and will definitely give you a chocolate high! You can try having a thin wedge of this, but I promise you'll be back for a second!

Serves
6

Temperature
350°F

Cooking Time
55 minutes

¼ cup unsalted butter, softened

½ cup sugar

2 eggs

1 teaspoon vanilla

1¼ cups Nutella® (or other chocolate hazelnut spread), divided

¼ cup flour

1 teaspoon baking powder

¼ teaspoon salt

dark chocolate fudge topping

coarsely chopped toasted hazelnuts

1. Cream the butter and sugar together with an electric hand mixer until light and fluffy. Add the eggs, vanilla, and ¾ cup of the Nutella® and mix until combined. Combine the flour, baking powder and salt together, and add these dry ingredients to the butter mixture, beating for 1 minute.

2. Pre-heat the air fryer to 350ºF.

3. Grease a 7-inch cake pan with butter and then line the bottom of the pan with a circle of parchment paper. Grease the parchment paper circle as well. Pour the batter into the prepared cake pan and wrap the pan completely with aluminum foil. Lower the pan into the air fryer basket with an aluminum sling (fold a piece of aluminum foil into a strip about 2-inches wide by 24-inches long). Fold the ends of the aluminum foil over the top of the dish before returning the basket to the air fryer. Air-fry for 30 minutes. Remove the foil and air-fry for another 25 minutes.

4. Remove the cake from air fryer and let it cool for 10 minutes. Invert the cake onto a plate, remove the parchment paper and invert the cake back onto a serving platter. While the cake is still warm, spread the remaining ½ cup of Nutella® over the top of the cake. Melt the dark chocolate fudge in the microwave for about 10 seconds so it melts enough to be pourable. Drizzle the sauce on top of the cake in a zigzag motion. Turn the cake 90 degrees and drizzle more sauce in zigzags perpendicular to the first zigzags. Garnish the edges of the torte with the toasted hazelnuts and serve.

A Little More

Bacon

The air fryer cooks bacon so nicely. It's contained so there's no splatter anywhere in your kitchen and the bacon crisps quickly because all the rendered fat drops into the basket below. If you want to cook strips of bacon, you'll be limited a little by the space you have to lay the strips out. If, however, you chop the bacon into pieces, you can cook more at one time – just remember to shake the basket every once in a while to redistribute the bacon.

Makes
4 strips of bacon

Temperature
400°F

Cooking Time
5 to 7 minutes

4 strips or ¼ pound bacon

1. Pre-heat the air fryer to 400°F.

2. Cut the strips of bacon to fit the air fryer basket, or chop the bacon up into pieces.

3. Pour a little water into the bottom drawer of the air fryer. This is to catch the grease that will render off the bacon. Transfer the bacon to the air fryer basket and air-fry for 5 to 7 minutes, depending on how crisp you would like your bacon. If you're cooking chopped bacon, shake the basket once or twice during the cooking process to help the bacon cook evenly.

Roasted Onions

It's nice to have an alternate method to browning onions, rather than always sautéing them on the stovetop. In the air fryer, there's no splatter from the onions and your stovetop is free to do other things. Whether you need them to mix into hamburgers, or a frittata, or to top a crostini, doing them in the air fryer will be quick and painless.

Makes
1 cup

Temperature
350°F

Cooking Time
10 to 15 minutes

1 onion, sliced or cut into ¾-inch chunks

olive oil

salt and freshly ground black pepper

1. Pre-heat the air fryer to 350°F.

2. Toss the onion in a bowl with a little olive oil, salt and freshly ground black pepper.

3. Transfer the onion to the air fryer basket and air-fry for 10 to 15 minutes (depending on how tender you'd like them to be), shaking the basket a few times during the cooking process.

Roasted Bell Pepper

Roasting a pepper in the air fryer is so easy and makes no mess at all. Just remember to turn the pepper as the skin blackens.

Makes
2 peppers

Temperature
400°F

Cooking Time
18 to 20 minutes

2 bell peppers
(red, orange, yellow or green)

1. Pre-heat the air fryer to 400°F.

2. Place the peppers in the air-fryer basket and air-fry for 18 to 20 minutes, rotating the peppers every 5 minutes throughout the cooking process as the skins start to blacken.

3. When the skins are black all over, remove the peppers from the air fryer and place on a plate to cool. Inverting a bowl over the peppers helps steam the peppers a little as they cool. Although this slows the cooling process slightly, it does make the skins easier to peel.

Roasted Garlic

Roasted garlic makes a nice addition to so many dishes – mashed potatoes, a mayonnaise, a salad dressing. Now there's no need to heat up your large oven to roast a head of garlic. The air fryer can do it in just 15 minutes.

Makes
1 head

Temperature
380°F

Cooking Time
15 minutes

1 head garlic

olive oil

salt

1. Pre-heat the air fryer to 380°F.

2. Slice off the top of the head of garlic to expose the tops of all the cloves.

3. Drizzle a little olive oil on the top of the garlic head and season with salt.

4. Place the head of garlic, cut side up, into the air fryer basket. Air-fry for 15 minutes.

5. When finished, let the garlic cool a little and then squeeze out the roasted garlic cloves.

Fried Tofu

Tofu works so perfectly in the air fryer that I couldn't leave it out of the book. Cut into cubes, it absorbs the flavor of the marinade quickly and then crisps beautifully in the air fryer. Add it to a salad or your favorite noodle dish, like Pad Thai! You can use any marinade that you like. Here's one to get you started.

Serves
2

Temperature
400°F

Cooking Time
10 to 15 minutes

1 pound firm or extra firm tofu

1 tablespoon canola oil

1 tablespoon rice vinegar

1 tablespoon sriracha chili sauce

3 tablespoons soy sauce

1 teaspoon toasted sesame oil

minced garlic or ginger, to taste

1. Cut the tofu into cubes. Mix the remaining ingredients in a bowl and toss the tofu in gently. Let the tofu marinate for 10 minutes.

2. Pre-heat the air fryer to 400°F.

3. Remove the tofu cubes from the marinade with a slotted spoon and transfer them to the air fryer. Air-fry for 10 to 15 minutes, depending on how crispy you want the tofu to be. Shake the basket once or twice during the cooking time to redistribute the tofu cubes. When they are crispy to your liking, remove and enjoy!

Toasted Nuts

The timing on this recipe depends on two things – which nuts are you toasting and how toasted you want them to be. So, be sure to open the air fryer during the cooking time to check to see how the toasting is progressing.

Makes
1 cup

Temperature
350°F

Cooking Time
3 to 5 minutes

1 cup nuts
(almonds, walnuts, hazelnuts, pecans, pine nuts)

1. Pre-heat the air fryer to 350°F.

2. Transfer the nuts to the air fryer basket and air fry for 3 to 5 minutes, depending on the nut and how toasted you would like the nuts. Shake the basket a few times during the cooking process.

3. If toasting really small nuts, like pine nuts that might fall through the holes in the air fryer basket, put them into a little cake pan and place the cake pan into the air fryer basket. Shake the pan to redistribute the nuts halfway through the cooking process.

Blue Jean Chef Pizza Dough

This pizza dough recipe is great for the calzone and stromboli recipes in the book. If you're making stromboli, divide the dough in half and make 2 stromboli. If you're making calzones, divide the dough into three equal portions. For individual pizzas, divide the dough into 6 portions.

4 cups bread flour, pizza ("00") flour or all-purpose flour

1 teaspoons active dry yeast

2 teaspoons sugar

2 teaspoons salt

1½ cups water

1 tablespoon olive oil

1. Combine the flour, yeast, sugar and salt in the bowl of a stand mixer. Add the olive oil to the flour mixture and start to mix using the dough hook attachment. As you're mixing, add 1¼ cups of the water, mixing until the dough comes together. Continue to knead the dough with the dough hook for another 10 minutes, adding enough water to get the right dough consistency.

2. Transfer the dough to a floured counter and divide it into the desired portion size. Roll each portion into a ball. Lightly coat each dough ball with oil and transfer to the refrigerator, covered with plastic wrap. You can place them all on a baking sheet, or place each dough ball into its own oiled zipper sealable plastic bag or container. (You can freeze the dough balls at this stage, removing as much air as possible from the oiled bag.) Keep in the refrigerator for at least one day, or as long as five days.

3. When you're ready to make your calzone, stromboli or pizza remove your pizza dough from the refrigerator at least 1 hour prior to air-frying and let it sit on the counter, covered gently with plastic wrap.

Corn Tortilla Chips

If you have extra tortillas around, this is a great way to use them up. It's also a great way to portion control your chip intake, if you're anything like me! Fry up only as many as you will let yourself eat and have fresh chips every time.

Makes
as many as you let yourself have

Temperature
380°F

Cooking Time
5 minutes

10- or 8-inch corn tortilla, cut into wedges

1 teaspoon vegetable oil

salt

1. Pre-heat the air fryer to 380°F.

2. Spray or brush the tortilla triangles with the oil and transfer them to the air fryer basket. Don't overfill the air fryer basket, but fry in batches. Air-fry for 5 minutes. Shake the basket once or twice during the cooking time to redistribute the ingredients.

3. Season the chips with salt as soon as they are finished.

Index

Index

Index

Index

Meredith's Cookbooks

Fast Favorites Under Pressure

Fast Favorites Under Pressure offers over 120 recipes, tips and tricks to help you be successful with your 4-quart pressure cooker. With recipes for soups, pastas, meats and seafood, grains, vegetarian entrées and desserts, there's a way for every eater to get a meal on the table in a fraction of the time.

Delicious Under Pressure

Delicious Under Pressure is Meredith's second pressure cooker cookbook that is full of easy, flavorful, and unexpected pressure cooker recipes. With 131 recipes, over 110 photos and all new chapters on Vegetarian Main Courses and Breakfast Dishes, it's a must-have cookbook for pressure-cooking at any level.

Comfortable Under Pressure

If your pressure cooker has been collecting dust, then you need to get Comfortable Under Pressure! With 125 recipes and over 100 tips and explanations, Blue Jean Chef: Comfortable Under Pressure will help you create delicious meals while becoming more versatile and at ease with your pressure cooker.

Comfortable in the Kitchen

Are you as comfortable in the kitchen as you are in your blue jeans? In Blue Jean Chef: Comfortable in the Kitchen, Meredith helps you settle into your comfort zone in the kitchen with 200 kitchen-tested recipes, tips, tricks and explanations of cooking techniques. Each chapter contains basic recipes that will give you a solid understanding of how the dish works, and four other recipes that build on that technique, but use different ingredients to create a unique and delicious meal.

Air Fryer Cooking Chart

NOTE: All times and temperatures below assume that the food is flipped over half way through the cooking time or the basket is shaken to redistribute ingredients once or twice.

Vegetables

	Temperature (°F)	Time (min)		Temperature (°F)	Time (min)
Asparagus (sliced 1-inch)	400°F	5	Onions (pearl)	400°F	10
Beets (whole)	400°F	40	Parsnips (½-inch chunks)	380°F	15
Broccoli (florets)	400°F	6	Peppers (1-inch chunks)	400°F	15
Brussels Sprouts (halved)	380°F	15	Potatoes (small baby, 1.5 lbs)	400°F	15
Carrots (sliced ½-inch)	380°F	15	Potatoes (1-inch chunks)	400°F	12
Cauliflower (florets)	400°F	12	Potatoes (baked whole)	400°F	40
Corn on the cob	390°F	6	Squash (½-inch chunks)	400°F	12
Eggplant (1½-inch cubes)	400°F	15	Sweet Potato (baked)	380°F	30 to 35
Fennel (quartered)	370°F	15	Tomatoes (cherry)	400°F	4
Green Beans	400°F	5	Tomatoes (halves)	350°F	10
Kale leaves	250°F	12	Zucchini (½-inch sticks)	400°F	12
Mushrooms (sliced ¼-inch)	400°F	5			

Chicken

	Temperature (°F)	Time (min)		Temperature (°F)	Time (min)
Breasts, bone in (1.25 lbs.)	370°F	25	Legs, bone in (1.75 lbs.)	380°F	30
Breasts, boneless (4 oz.)	380°F	12	Wings (2 lbs.)	400°F	12
Drumsticks (2.5 lbs.)	370°F	20	Game Hen (halved - 2 lbs.)	390°F	20
Thighs, bone in (2 lbs.)	380°F	22	Whole Chicken (6.5 lbs.)	360°F	75
Thighs, boneless (1.5 lbs.)	380°F	18 to 20	Tenders	360°F	8 to 10

Beef

	Temperature (°F)	Time (min)		Temperature (°F)	Time (min)
Burger (4 oz.)	370°F	16 to 20	Meatballs (3-inch)	380°F	10
Filet Mignon (8 oz.)	400°F	18	Ribeye, bone in (1-inch, 8 oz.)	400°F	10 to 15
Flank Steak (1.5 lbs.)	400°F	12	Sirloin steaks (1-inch, 12 oz.)	400°F	9 to 14
London Broil (2 lbs.)	400°F	20 to 28	Beef Eye Round Roast (4 lbs.)	390°F	45 to 55
Meatballs (1-inch)	380°F	7			